636
FE

Fenton, Carroll Lane

Animals that help us

DATE			
JUN 25			
DEC 17			
JUN 8			
MAR 4 1990			

Animals That Help Us

THIS book is one in a series that tells the stories of living things which human beings raise and use or keep as pets. Other volumes include *Fruits We Eat* and *Plants We Live On.*

Every one of us knows some domestic animals, which have warm blood and hair, and therefore should be called mammals. The smallest are guinea pigs; the largest are cattle and work horses weighing a ton or more. The strangest probably are camels and llamas, but cattle are the most useful. Elephants, which are bigger than horses and stranger than camels, are not really domesticated. But they are such important work animals that they have their place in this book.

In this new edition of *Animals That Help Us*, which has been through seven previous printings since its original publication, the text has been thoroughly revised to incorporate the latest findings of science. Altogether there are changes on about one-third of the pages of text. There is extensive new material, now placed in a separate chapter, on the arctic reindeer and musk oxen. Information about new types of animals being bred, such as the zorses and zebroids of East Africa, is incorporated, as well as new data on wild animals. Datings of species are revised in the light of current knowledge.

Man has used domestic animals for thousands of years—ever since the latter part of the Stone Age. But which ones did he use first, and where did he get them? What did early types look like, and how did they differ from breeds that are common today? How did the creatures spread from continent to continent? Are new breeds still being developed, and why are they better than those we have known for years? *Animals That Help Us* answers these questions and many more.

Domestic animals and their wild ancestors appear in fifty-five illustrations containing more than seventy of Dr. Fenton's drawings.

Mrs. Kitchen, who completed this revision just before her recent death, was a writer on agricultural subjects and for many years associate editor of the international magazine *Soil Science.* The late Dr. Fenton was widely known as an author and illustrator in many fields of science.

Animals
That Help Us

The Story of Domestic Animals

Revised Edition

By CARROLL LANE FENTON
and HERMINIE B. KITCHEN

Illustrated by Carroll Lane Fenton

The John Day Company   *New York*
An Intext Publisher

The John Day Company, 257 Park Avenue South, New York, N.Y. 10010

Published on the same day in Canada by Longman Canada Limited.

Printed in the United States of America

First published 1959
Ninth impression, 1974
Revised edition 1973

Library of Congress Cataloging in Publication Data

Fenton, Carroll Lane, 1900- 1969
   Animals that help us.

   SUMMARY: Discusses the way various animals became domesticated and their uses to man. Includes dogs, sheep, horses, reindeer, elephants, and others.
    1. Domestic animals---Juvenile literature.
[1. Domestic animals] I. Kitchen, Herminie Broedel, 1901-1973   joint author. II. Title.
SF75.5.F4 1973   636   73-642
ISBN 0-381-99822-3

Contents

Eohippus (right), the dawn horse, lived about 50 million years ago. Various kinds were 10 to 20 inches high.

Mesohippus (left), a three-toed horse, lived some 35 million years ago. Height at the shoulder, 24 to 30 inches.

A modern Arabian horse. Height 5 feet, or 15 hands.

Three stages in the development of horses.

Wild, Tame, and Domesticated

WHEN the first human beings wanted to travel, they had to go on foot. When they gathered firewood, they carried it home. When they were hungry, they ate wild plants or hunted wild animals. They had no domestic animals to provide them with meat or to help them do their work.

This went on for thousands and thousands of years — longer than we can imagine. But about 11,000 years ago, people in southwest Asia began to gather and store supplies of wild food plants and bring home live animals. Later, they built permanent homes and began to grow grains and other plants and tame the animals.

No one *knows* how animals were first tamed, but we *think* they were kept as pets. Hunters probably killed wild dogs or jackals, and took their puppies home. Other hunters took home lambs, kids, calves, pigs, colts, and baby donkeys.

In time, animals kept as pets also became useful. Small puppies were fun to play with, but grown-up dogs helped their masters hunt rabbits and other game. Calves and donkeys carried loads. Donkeys could be ridden, too, and so could young horses that were accustomed to children. Sheep, goats, and pigs could be killed and eaten when wild food became scarce.

At first these animals were tamed, not domesticated. A tame animal is a creature that has been kept and fed and petted, until it is willing to live with people. But it still is like its wild rela-

7

tives and can easily go back to a wild life if set free.

Domestic animals have been kept and cared for so long that they have become different from their wild ancestors. Wild jackals, for example, were small, timid animals, and so were those that hunters first tamed. But domesticated jackals became larger, braver, and more friendly as they turned into dogs. Wild sheep had straight hair and short tails, and were able to take care of themselves. The tails of domestic sheep became long, and several types developed wool. The animals also became so dull and timid that all except one breed *must* be cared for by human beings. Cats and most dogs can still run wild, but they have developed shapes, colors, and habits which are very different from those of wild cats, dogs, and jackals.

Domestic animals that run away from their homes do not become exactly like their wild ancestors. To show that they are different, we use another word for them: feral (fee′ral). Dogs and cats often become feral. So do horses, goats, pigs, and cattle.

An ancient Egyptian with a domestic ibex. At the right is a goat.

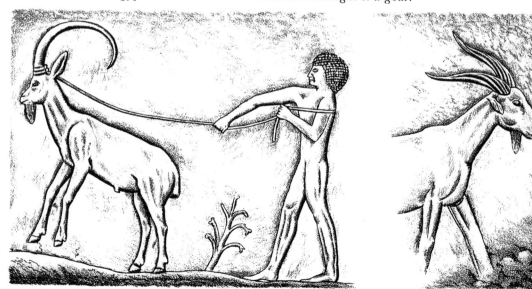

Egyptian herdsman with gazelle (left) and addax antelope (right).

Ancient people kept all sorts of animals as pets, and they domesticated some that are not kept today or reverted to the wild and have only lately been domesticated again. Carvings and paintings show that ancient Egyptians tamed or domesticated the lynx, which is related to our wild bobcat. Egyptians also had herds of gazelles, ibexes, and addax antelopes. Today on game ranches in Kenya and Rhodesia, elands, oryx, and other antelopes that have been wild since the days of ancient Egypt are being domesticated again and raised for meat and hides on land where cattle cannot find enough feed and water. People of Sumer drove small horses called kiangs, though all kiangs are now wild.

No one knows why ancient Sumerians and Egyptians stopped raising these animals. Perhaps the animals did not work as hard or produce as much meat as horses, cattle, sheep, and the other animals that are still domesticated and whose stories are told in this book.

Dogs Came First

PEPPER pushed at the kitchen door till it opened, and went out on the porch. There he wagged his tail and looked at the cat, but she paid no attention to him. Pepper left her and trotted about the farmyard. When he came to the lane, or driveway, that led to the road, he lay down on the ground with his muzzle between his paws.

Pepper was a shepherd dog, though he was sometimes called a Border Collie. He was smaller than true collies, however, for he was about 18 inches high at the shoulder, and collies are 22 to 24 inches. Pepper had shaggy black-and-white hair, with a few tan marks on his chest. The hair had made him so warm that he panted to cool himself. He did this by opening his mouth and taking deep, rapid breaths. Dogs cannot cool themselves by perspiring, or sweating, as horses and people do.

Pepper lay down because he was waiting for his master, Craig, to come home from school. Although the dog could not "read" a clock, he had some way of telling time. He always went to the lane a few minutes before the yellow school bus would come down the road.

Pepper lay still until he heard the bus, which sounded different from passenger cars or trucks. Then the dog jumped up and

Pepper, the shepherd dog, is also called Border Collie.

ran down the lane. He was waiting at the road when the bus stopped. As Craig stepped out, Pepper barked loudly. "Don't make so much noise," Craig told him. "Come on — I'll race you to the house!"

The boy and dog played games for a while, and then they did their chores. First they went to a pasture to look at the sheep and to find a lamb that had wandered away from its mother. Then Craig and Pepper went to another pasture to round up the cows and drive them to the barn to be milked. When two cows began to quarrel, Pepper barked at them until they stopped. He also barked at a cow that paused to eat grass. "No more of that!" he seemed to be saying. "Go along with the other cows!"

.   .   .

Dogs were the first domestic animals, but people have not always had them. If we could visit the caves where human beings lived during very ancient times, we would find no trace of domestic dogs. We also would find no trace of domestic sheep or cattle for dogs to watch over and herd. In those times all

Stone-age painting of a man hunting a deer. The animal behind it is a dog.

animals were wild, and hunters killed them in pitfalls or with spears and axes of stone.

These ancient ways began to change about 11,000 years ago. Some tribes learned to hunt with bows and arrows, which could be shot much farther than spears could be thrown. Other tribes tracked game with the help of wolflike dogs, which also kept beasts such as wild boars from attacking their masters. Still other tribes settled on northern seacoasts, where they hunted and fished but also ate oysters, clams, and cockles. These people tossed bones, empty shells, and other rubbish into piles which we now call kitchen middens.

Scientists dig into kitchen middens to discover how people lived thousands of years ago. The scientists find weapons, tools, and small things such as fishhooks which were thrown away or lost. There also are skulls and bones of small dogs, about 15 inches high at the shoulder. The animals were much like yellowish-gray wild dogs, or jackals, which once ranged from Denmark to Asia. They still are found in southeastern Europe

An Egyptian greyhound (left) and a jackal (right) of the type once found in Europe.

and Turkey, though they are becoming scarce in many places.

People of the kitchen middens tamed jackals, and so did tribes that lived in southern France and several other parts of Europe. The animals gave warning when bears, wolves, or human beings tried to approach a camp. Many modern dogs also have this habit of making a noise when strangers come near.

Soon after jackal-dogs became common, larger types appeared. They were developed from a wild kind, or species (spee' sheez), that probably lived in Asia. Scientists have named it *Canis familiaris,* which means "family, or domestic, dog." The wild species has disappeared. It either died out or mixed with domesticated strains thousands of years ago.

Four varieties of *Canis familiaris* were tamed, probably in different regions. These four varieties produced the groups of dogs that are most important today. A few other types were developed from other wild species that lived in southeastern Asia and in America.

13

One variety of the wild dog was a rather short-legged animal. In Asia it produced dogs of three sorts. The ancient Chinese, for example, had hunting dogs, watchdogs, and dogs that were eaten as medicine. The meat of yellow-haired dogs was supposed to cure tuberculosis. Dog hearts were eaten to stop nosebleed and to cure rheumatism.

The ancient Egyptians domesticated a slender, long-necked variety of dog. About 6,000 years ago, some descendants of these

Four varieties of wild dogs, with the names of some of their descendants.

Greyhounds, Beagle, Great Dane   *Spaniels, setters, Eskimo Dog*

Collie, German Shepherd, Border Collie   *Boxer, mastiffs, St. Bernard*

wild animals became the first greyhounds. They were spotted animals with pointed heads, short hair, and tails that curved upward. Their stiff ears could be laid back or raised when the dogs were alert.

These early greyhounds were the most important dogs in Egypt for more than 3,000 years. But other sorts became common, too. One, now called the Saluki, was almost as slender as the greyhound but had drooping ears and longer hair. Another looked rather like a terrier with erect ears and short tail curled over the back. Egyptian house dogs were short-legged relatives of Chinese dogs and the modern spaniel. In ancient paintings they look almost like our modern Dachshunds.

Mastiffs came from a third variety of the "family" wild dog. This variety was larger than the others. The domestic dogs that have come from it include two or three kinds of mastiff, St. Bernards, Boxers, Great Danes, and other big breeds.

The fourth variety of the "family" wild dog was as big as the one that produced mastiffs. In western Asia this creature became a sheepdog, and was used to take care of flocks. As thousands of years went by, sheepdogs produced collies and shepherds of various kinds. Pepper was one of the modern dogs descended from this wild variety.

. . .

The kitchen-midden people kept jackal pups as pets, and young sheepdogs were fine playmates for children. The Egyptians kept dogs in their houses as pets and used them outdoors for hunting. Greyhounds and Salukis ran down antelopes or caught them at waterholes. Mastiffs were used to hunt lions,

Cocker Spaniel

Beagle

Dachshund

Boxer

Collie

Five popular breeds of dogs.

leopards, and other animals. The Egyptians also trained spotted hyenas to hunt. The hyenas were tamed and trained, but were not domesticated. They were kept in wooden cages.

Egyptians were very fond of their dogs. The animals were sacred to one of the gods, and people believed that he sometimes came to earth in the body of a dog. Pictures of dogs were carved or painted on the walls of temples. When a rich man's favorite dog died, the whole family went into mourning. The dead animal was made into a mummy and was buried in a cemetery especially reserved for dogs.

Most ancient dogs were loyal and friendly, but the big mastiffs from central Asia had bad tempers. Armies of ancient Babylonia, Assyria, and Greece used these fierce animals in war. The Romans also trained mastiffs to run in bands and attack the enemy. Other Roman war dogs kept watch in towers or carried messages fastened to their collars.

The Romans, like the ancient Chinese, had three classes of dog. In the first class were sporting dogs. They were used in war and hunting, and the fiercest types fought in arenas against human gladiators. House dogs were both pets and watchdogs, but shepherds cared for cattle and sheep. Shepherd dogs often wore broad spiked collars to protect them from wolves.

The Gauls, who often fought Roman armies, put curved blades as well as spikes on the collars of their war dogs. When the dogs dashed through enemy cavalry, the blades cut the horses' legs. Later, during the Middle Ages, both knights and their horses wore armor. War dogs also were given armor made of steel plates, chain mail, and canvas. Only big, strong animals could run with such heavy coats of armor.

An Egyptian wolfhound (left) and a Saluki (right), a very old breed.

Dogs were taken to the British Isles from the mainland of Europe and from western Asia. Some types became tall hounds that hunted deer and killed wolves. Others were war mastiffs that fought against both cavalry and soldiers on foot. By the year A.D. 800, Saxon chieftains used greyhounds to run down deer. A hundred years later, laws decreed that only nobles and gentlemen might keep greyhounds for hunting. Common people who lived around forests were allowed to keep shepherd dogs and certain pet dogs. But anyone who owned a large dog, such as a hound or mastiff, had to make it lame by cutting tendons in its "knees." This kept it from chasing the nobleman's deer.

As years went by, dogs were bred for special purposes. Shepherds, collies, and sheepdogs herded sheep. Pointers hunted game birds by smell, and pointed toward the birds with their muzzles. Corgies were kept to drive cattle out of fields and pastures where they did not belong. Short-legged Dachshunds followed badgers into their holes. Boxers became good fighters

18

with other dogs and with bulls. Bulldogs also were bred to fight. Their snub noses let them breathe even while they clung to the throat or muzzle of a bull.

.   .   .

We say a great deal about dogs as pets and as hunters, but they also pull carts and sleds. In Europe, St. Bernards, Great Danes, and other big dogs often pull two-wheeled carts loaded with vegetables, cans of milk, or even hay. Eskimo dogs and Siberian Huskies are famous for hauling sleds in the North, where there are no roads and the ground is covered with snow for more than half of the year.

Both Eskimo dogs and Huskies seem to be descended from ancient Samoyedes. Samoyedes are white animals with bushy tails that curl over their backs. Their undercoats, which are almost as soft as wool, are covered by long, coarse hair.

Samoyedes came from the same variety of wild dog that produced spaniels, setters, and pointers. Samoyedes were first bred to herd reindeer in Siberia, but they also were trained to pull sleds. Samoyedes are related to Chow Chows and Spitzes, two breeds that are now kept as pets.

The Husky is a soft-haired dog from northern Siberia. Although it is not very large, it can run very fast and is often used in races. It is more friendly than other sled dogs, and puppies make fine pets.

The Eskimo is a big, strong dog that also came from Siberia, but was brought to North America and Greenland hundreds of years ago. Eskimos use these dogs to hunt polar bears and musk oxen as well as to pull sleds.

Alaskan Malamutes are large sled dogs, too. They are nearly two feet high at the shoulder and weigh almost 70 pounds. This breed probably began when Huskies were mated to big gray wolves of Alaska. Both Malamutes and Huskies also are used as pack animals. The dogs carry loads through forests and over mountains where they could not pull sleds.

Some American Indian dogs must have begun as coyotes, which are small, clever wolves. But in the days before horses became common, Indians of the West had dogs larger than Malamutes. These big dogs carried packs, but they also were harnessed to the travois (trah′ vwah). This was a frame of poles that crossed above the dog's back, with its other ends on the ground. Clothing, baskets, and even children were put on the travois, which the dog dragged across the plains when the people moved.

The Siberian Husky is a speedy sled dog that makes a friendly pet.

Indians of Mexico had small dogs that probably were brought from Asia thousands of years ago. One variety, called the techichi (teh chee' chee), was plump and bowlegged, with gray skin and almost no hair. Techichis were kept in pens and were fattened and eaten, for the ancient Mexicans had no cattle, sheep, or other large "meat" animals. Even in South America, where there were herds of llamas, the Indians often ate fat dogs.

.   .   .

Most of the breeds of dogs in America today came by way of Europe. Spanish conquerors brought hounds and other hunting dogs to Mexico and South America. Two dogs came from England on the *Mayflower*. One was a spaniel and the other a Mastiff. In time, other breeds of dogs were brought to the New World and new breeds were developed in the United States. Among these are the Chesapeake Bay Retriever, the American Water Spaniel, and the Boston Terrier.

There are about 25 million dogs in the United States today, with more millions in Canada, Mexico, and other countries of the Americas. Many of these dogs are purebred, which means that they belong to just one breed. In fact, more than 100 breeds of dogs are recognized by the American Kennel Club. Other dogs are not quite pure, and millions are ordinary mongrels. They are descended from dogs of various breeds, which mated just as they wanted to. Mongrels can never win prizes in a dog show, but they do very well as watchdogs, hunters, and pets.

Sheep for Meat and Wool

"BAH-AH-AH!" said a lamb in a shaky voice as he trotted behind his mother. When she paused, he came close to her and rubbed against her side.

The lamb and his mother belonged to a flock that lived in a grassy pasture. The lamb was so timid that he never felt safe unless he was near his mother. He liked other company, too, and Mother always stayed with the rest of the flock.

The sheep had coats of white wool, but their muzzles and legs were dark brown. Wool made the animals seem larger than they really were. Each mother, or ewe (yoo), was about two feet high and weighed almost 180 pounds. The males, or rams, which were a few inches taller, weighed about 200 pounds.

The sheep walked about with their heads near the ground, nibbling the crisp green grass. Suddenly they heard angry barking and snarling. Pepper, the shepherd dog, had found two strange dogs in the pasture and was driving them away.

The lamb's mother looked up in alarm. "Bah-ah-ah-ah!" she bleated loudly. Then she began to run. Other ewes also bleated and ran. Soon the whole flock was dashing across the pasture, leaving the lamb behind.

The strange dogs tried to follow the sheep, but Pepper drove them away. Then he ran ahead of the flock, which was galloping toward a barbed-wire fence. Pepper had to bark and even snap at the animals to keep them from running into the fence. One ewe did dart past him and cut herself on the barbed wire.

.   .   .

Dogs were the first domestic animals, and scientists who once thought sheep were the second, now believe this place should go to goats. We know that almost 9,000 years ago, Stone-age tribes of western Asia owned small flocks of sheep. And about 8,500 years ago, people who built a town in the country now called Iraq (ee rahk´) grew wheat and kept dogs, pigs, cattle, and animals that seem to have been about halfway between sheep and goats.

Stone-age people domesticated wild sheep of two or three different kinds. The first of these, called mouflon (moof´ lon), still

Some domestic sheep came from the wild mouflon.

lives on islands near Italy and among mountains in southwestern Asia. Mouflons are a little more than two feet high at the shoulder; though the rams have big coiled horns, the ewes are hornless. The animals have reddish-brown hair with a lighter patch on each side of the body. The hair covers short underwool that keeps the mouflons warm in winter.

The urial (oo´ ri al) is a larger wild sheep that lives on grassy hills and plains from Persia to central Asia. Urials stand 30 to 36 inches high and are covered with brownish-gray hair that becomes lighter in summer. The rams develop big coiled horns, but the horns of ewes remain small.

Argali (ar´ ga li) sheep live among the mountains of Mongolia and Tibet, in central Asia. The animals have gray-brown hair and sometimes become four feet high. Some scientists think domestic sheep of Mongolia and Tibet are partly descended from argalis. Others say the domestic animals came from urials, which produced most of the domestic sheep that are common today.

Wild sheep have hair, short tails, and horns, and their ears do not droop. But as the animals were domesticated, they began to change. The sheep kept by Stone-age farmers in Iraq had tails that reached halfway to the ground. The horns twisted and spread sideways, and the ears probably drooped. Sheep of this kind were taken to Europe about 6,000 years ago. The European animals are often called "peat sheep" because their bones have been found in beds of half-decayed plants, or peat, that settled on the bottoms of swamps.

Almost 6,000 years ago, Egyptian artists carved pictures of sheep on the stone wall of a temple. These animals had long

An Egyptian picture of a hairy sheep, and the living animal.

legs and short hair on the body, though long hair hung down from the throat and chest. Both rams and ewes had twisted horns that extended sideways but did not curl.

Later pictures show Egyptian farmers driving flocks of these long-legged sheep through their fields, to tramp seed grain into the ground. In time, the peat sheep also were brought to Egypt. Still later (about 2,700 years ago), the Egyptians obtained sheep with wool instead of hair. When this new breed became common the old hairy sheep disappeared.

The same thing happened in Europe, when people who built towns over lakes first raised hairy peat sheep. Then, about 2,500 years ago, the Lake Dwellers began to keep woolly sheep with short tails. These animals were probably developed from newly tamed mouflons, and came from southwestern Asia. Although the wool was short and thin, the Lake Dwellers liked it so well that they stopped breeding peat sheep. In time, this old, hairy breed died out, but short-wooled sheep are still raised on islands northwest of Scotland. They are almost the only domestic sheep that can run wild, or become feral. Other breeds never learn to take care of themselves.

The early tribes of Israel kept sheep for both meat and wool. The favorite meat was tails of fat-tailed sheep, which had appeared in Babylonia 5,000 years ago. These animals, which probably came from urials, had shaggy hair, drooping ears, and tails that weighed 10 to 20 pounds. Some modern breeds have tails that divide into two thick parts.

In the days before money was invented, people paid for things with sheep and other domestic animals. The first silver coins are supposed to have been worth one sheep each. These coins were used in western Asia about 700 years before Jesus was born. Even today, some of the people in central Asia figure prices in year-old lambs.

. . .

As time went by, farmers began to raise sheep with longer and better wool. These animals did not come from the mouflon or from the short-wooled sheep of Europe. The new breeds

Fat-tailed sheep (left) and a Columbia sheep (right). The Columbia is a modern breed developed in Idaho, especially for life in the West.

were descended from urials, and they were developed in countries near the eastern end of the Mediterranean Sea. From there they were taken to other regions. About 2,700 years ago, Phoenician traders took long-wooled sheep to northern Africa, Italy, and Spain.

The Romans conquered Spain about 2,100 years ago. Though Spain already had long-wooled sheep, the Romans soon brought improved breeds of their own. The most famous of these came from Tarentum, but fine rams also were brought from Roman colonies in Africa. When these animals were interbred, Spanish sheep developed the best coats of wool in Europe.

Most sheep were raised for meat and wool, but some were bred for milking. Such sheep were common in ancient times, and a few are important today. A ewe of one breed, called the Friesian, produces as much as 1,100 pounds of milk a year, or about 550 quarts. Imported Roquefort (roke' fort) cheese is made from sheep's milk. Herds of milk sheep live on farms near the town of Roquefort, France, from which the cheese gets its name.

The first English sheep were hairy, like those of ancient Egypt. Then came short-wooled sheep like those of the Lake Dwellers. Still later, British farmers began to improve their flocks by bringing high-grade animals from Spain and other countries on the mainland of Europe. At last, about 700 years ago, British sheep became so good that long-fleeced rams were sent from England to improve the breeds that had been developed in Spain.

Huge flocks of sheep were owned by Spanish noblemen. Every spring the animals were driven from their winter pastures in valleys to summer grazing lands on the mountains. Officials called merinos (meh ree′ noz) decided where each flock should graze. Long before Columbus discovered America, Spaniards developed sheep that had long wool, stayed in close flocks, and were good travelers. In time this breed of sheep became known as the Merino.

Columbus brought Merino sheep on his second voyage to America. Other Spanish explorers took the animals to Mexico and California. English colonists brought sheep to Virginia in 1609, and to New England a few years later. In 1643, a mill was built in Massachusetts to weave woolen cloth.

After the American Revolution ended in 1781, Merino sheep were shipped from Spain to New York and New England.

Modern Merino sheep have short legs and long, fine wool.

Raising Merinos became the chief industry in Vermont, and by 1840 the state had more than five sheep to every human being. Settlers also took sheep when they moved westward to the Ohio and Mississippi valleys and then across the Great Plains of the West. Sheep raising became important in the Rocky Mountain states after 1869, when railroads reached them.

Many early western sheep were Merinos from Vermont. They had good wool, but their flesh was too strong to make good mutton. Many sheepmen got rid of Merinos and raised English sheep, which made good mutton and bore long wool.

Most Australian sheep are descended from Spanish Merinos, and so are the sheep of South Africa. But English breeds are commonest in Argentina, where many sheep are sold for mutton that is shipped to Europe and North America. Perhaps you have eaten canned mutton marked "Produce of Argentina."

Four types of sheep are raised in North America today. They are fine-wool, medium-wool, long-wool, and karakuls.

Fine-wool sheep began as Merinos. Modern American Merinos have shorter legs and longer bodies than those that first came from Spain. Some have deeply wrinkled skins and are bred only for their wool. Others, which have only a few wrinkles, provide both wool and mutton. The Rambouillet (ram boo yay') was developed in France during the 1700's from Merino ancestors. The Rambouillet is a hardy animal that is popular on plains of the West, where summer weather becomes very hot and winter weather grows very cold.

Medium-wool sheep are raised for both wool and mutton. Several breeds came from England and Scotland, but others were developed in the United States. Shropshires, which have dark brown muzzles, are the most popular farm sheep in North America. "Farm sheep" are kept in pastures instead of being herded on grassy plains, among mountains, or on deserts.

Long-wool sheep are big animals with coarse wool. They were developed for mutton in England and Scotland, but some breeds live very well on semideserts in the West. Others thrive in low, moist regions where there is plenty of rain.

Karakul sheep get their name from a town in south-central Asia. They are big, hardy animals that store fat in the upper part of the tail, which ends in a twisted point. The animals are bred for the skins of young lambs, which are covered with tightly curled hair. The type called broadtail is very silky, but Persian lamb is more tightly curled. Caracul (spelled with *C* not *K*) is the least beautiful and expensive.

A few Karakul sheep are raised in the State of New York, but most American flocks are in the West. Other sheep are common in the West, too, for Texas, California, and Colorado have more than any other states. Ontario, Quebec, and Alberta are the greatest sheep-raising provinces in Canada.

.   .   .

Wild sheep are strong, active animals that can take care of themselves, and so can the ancient short-wooled sheep that live on islands northwest of Scotland. But modern domestic sheep have become weak, stupid creatures that are easily frightened. Sheep that live in fenced pastures seldom get into trouble, but those that "run" across semideserts or among mountains must be guarded by men and dogs.

We often say that sheep run in flocks that are cared for by

shepherds. But in the western United States and Canada a flock of sheep is called a band, and the man who protects it is a sheep herder, not a shepherd.

Some herders walk behind their sheep and sleep in tents which they set up at night. These men put their tents and supplies on pack horses or burros, which travel with the sheep. But many western herders live in sheep wagons, which are hauled from one place to another by horses or by pickup trucks. A sheep wagon has four wheels which generally come from an old automobile and so have rubber tires. The specially built body contains one or two beds called bunks, as well as cupboards, lockers, and a stove. The curved top of the wagon is covered with aluminum or canvas, and there is a door at one end. In cold, rainy weather a sheep wagon is much more comfortable than a tent.

Goats

GOATS are closely related to sheep. They were tamed a little earlier, also somewhere in southwestern Asia.

Shall we imagine one of the first tame goats? It was an animal now called the pasang (pa sang´), a name that means "rock-footed." Pasangs are brownish-gray creatures about three feet high at the shoulder. Males have beards on their chins and long curved horns, but the females are beardless and their horns are short. Pasangs are sometimes found in low country, but they often live on mountains 10,000 to 12,000 feet high. The animals can run rapidly or leap from stone to stone.

A Stone-age hunter caught a baby pasang, or kid, that had wandered away from its mother. The man tied the little animal's legs and took it home to his children. They fed the kid and taught it to play. They also protected it from half-wild dogs that ran about the camp.

While this pasang was growing up, other hunters of the tribe also caught young ones. The animals fed and played together, and learned to chase the dogs instead of running from them. The dogs yelped and ran away when pasangs butted them with their foreheads and their rough-edged horns.

When these tame pasangs grew up, they mated and had

young ones, or kids, of their own. As this happened again and again, and year after year, the animals began to change. They became smaller than wild pasangs and developed shorter horns. The males, or billies, did not fight so much, and they did not want to run away. At last, between 8,000 and 9,000 years ago, the descendants of tame pasangs became domestic goats.

.　　.　　.

People who owned the first goats did not live in villages or on farms. They were hunters who roamed from one place to another, taking their goats with them. In time, the hunters traded goats for sheep, or for other goats with twisted horns. In this way the animals spread to Africa and Europe and across Asia. Goats reached Egypt about 6,000 years ago and entered Europe soon afterward. Chinese herdsmen began to raise goats about 4,000 years ago.

A wild pasang (left) and a modern Angora goat (right).

The first goats that were taken to Europe and Africa were small animals with short horns. They were raised both for meat and for milk. Lake Dwellers of Switzerland apparently kept goats in their houses and put the chalk-white milk into earthenware pots. These ancient animals gave much less than the three quarts of milk that are expected from a good milk goat today.

Ancient Egyptians kept flocks of goats. Farmers used them, as they used sheep, to trample seed grain into the ground. Goats of ancient Palestine were a variety of the pasang that had ears about 12 inches long. The animals often ran in the same flocks with sheep. The Israelites drank goat's milk and made cheese from it, and they liked the meat of kids better than mutton or lamb. Women made heavy cloth for tents out of goat hair, and skins were used as water bottles or for leather. Blown-up goatskins made swimming floats and buoys.

Goats also were sacrificed to God, and the "scapegoat" was part of the ceremony for the Day of Atonement. Priests put the people's sins on the head of a goat. Then the beast was driven out of the town and escaped to the wilderness.

Ancient carvings from Babylonia and Assyria show goats with long hair and horns that curved backward or pointed upward. Other carvings show fishermen in the water, riding on blown-up skins. Carvings made about 2,600 years ago show soldiers with goatskin floats swimming to attack a fort.

Pan was one of the gods worshiped by ancient Greeks and Romans. Pan had a goat's tail, hind legs, and feet, as well as goat's ears and short horns. Less important gods or spirits that resembled Pan were called fauns and satyrs.

Both Greeks and Romans ate kid meat, which still is popular

34

in Italy, Spain, and southern France, and on the island of Malta. There goats also supply most of the milk. They are led from house to house and are milked "to order."

Goat's-milk cheese is popular in Norway, Sweden, Switzerland, and several other countries of Europe. European farmers have raised milk goats for hundreds of years. The native goats have been mated with animals brought from other countries. The farmers also have selected good milk animals with special colors and other characteristics, and have bred them until special types were established.

.   .   .

Columbus brought goats as well as sheep on his second voyage to North America, but wild goats never lived on this continent. The shaggy white animal called a mountain goat, which lives in the West, really is an antelope related to the European ibex. Indians of the Northwest killed mountain goats for their wool and hair, but did not tame them.

Spanish settlers who came after Columbus brought milk goats to Mexico before 1550. In 1607, settlers from England also brought these animals to Virginia. "Wool" goats came from Europe more than 200 years later. Both types are now raised in the United States and Canada.

The Toggenburg is a popular milk goat that was developed in Switzerland. It was brought to North America in 1893. Toggenburgs have brown hair with white stripes on the face and white on the lower parts of the legs. Some animals have short hair, but the hair of others is long.

Saanen goats, which are white, also came from Switzerland.

They are large animals that sometimes give more than six quarts of milk a day. Both male and female Saanen goats have beards.

French Alpine goats resemble Saanens, but are black and white or black and pale brown. Anglo-Nubian goats have drooping ears and may be black, brown, tan, or spotted. As you can guess from the name, this breed first came from Africa. It was improved in England before it was brought to America.

Angora, or wool-bearing, goats first came to America from Turkey. They have drooping ears, silky hair, and twisted horns that become long on male animals. These horns may mean that the Angora is partly descended from wild goats that were different from pasangs. The domestic type is a very old one; Moses told his people to use goat's wool as well as silk when they wove altar cloths.

The white Saanen has been bred as a milk goat.

Angora goats thrive in Texas and other parts of the Southwest. They eat grass, weeds, and leaves from bushes or small trees. Ranchmen sometimes turn herds of Angora goats loose to clear pastures by eating bushes that grow there.

The fine, silky hair of Angora goats is called mohair. It is made into wigs for dolls and is woven into rugs, plush, and cloth for men's summer suits. About 130 years ago, mohair became so popular that Angora goats were mated with other kinds to increase the size of flocks. This produced bigger, stronger animals, but their hair is not as fine as that of old-time, purebred Angoras.

About four million Angora goats now live in the United States. If you see a flock of goats in the Southwest, you may be almost sure that they belong to this long-haired breed.

Goats are not as timid as sheep, and they do not become so badly frightened. This is why farmers often keep one or two goats with their sheep. The goats become leaders of the flock. They drive strange dogs out of the pasture and keep the sheep from running wildly or dashing into fences.

Horses, Large and Small

RUNNER chose his best spear and put his sharpest knife in his belt. "Are you ready?" he asked his brother. "We may have to go a long way before we find horses!"

Runner and his brother lived in France about 13,000 years ago, during the Old Stone Age. This was a time when people chipped weapons and tools from rocks such as flint. There were no domestic animals — not even dogs. Many tribes lived in shallow caves, but Runner's home was a hut covered with skin. Other skin huts stood near it, in a grassy valley.

The boys followed a trail that climbed a ridge and then crossed a plain. At last they saw a herd of wild horses grazing beside a creek.

Both Runner and his brother knew they had to be very careful, for horses were easily frightened. The boys slipped from one bush to another, and crawled slowly through the tall grass. Finally they separated. Runner hid behind a bush while his brother crept toward a young horse. It was a gray-brown animal less than four feet high at the shoulder. Its tail was almost black, and its dark mane stood up instead of drooping over its neck. The boys had their own name for it, but we call it a Celtic (selt´ ik) horse.

As Runner's brother crawled forward, the horse began to walk away. When it stopped, the boy crawled toward it again, guiding the animal toward Runner. At last it came close to the bush behind which he was hiding.

This was just what the boys wanted. Runner leaned back, aimed his spear, and drove it into the animal's body. The horse took one jump and fell dead as the boys shouted in triumph. They had killed a horse without any help! Now they could take its skin and meat to the village. This would prove that they were grown-up hunters who knew how to kill big game!

.   .   .

Many ancient hunters killed wild horses and feasted on their meat. The people tossed the bones on a pile behind their huts. As years passed, the pile grew larger and larger. At last it contained the bones of 100 thousand horses.

These were neither the world's first horses nor very ancient ones. The horse family is very old — much older than human beings. Its story began about 50 million years ago, when creatures which we now call eohippus (ee′ o hip′ us) lived in North America and Europe.

The name eohippus means "dawn horse" or "first horse," but these animals did not look like horses. Some species were about 10 inches high at the shoulder and weighed only a little more than some cats. Other kinds were 20 inches tall, or about as large as a foxhound. Their heads were long, their backs were arched, and their legs were slender. They had four toes on each front foot but only three behind.

Eohippus died out in Europe, leaving no known descendants.

At the left, a Stone-age drawing of a Celtic horse in its shaggy winter coat. At the right is a big, heavy-bodied forest horse.

American dawn horses also died out — but before that happened some species had young ones that were not quite like their parents. These creatures had young ones that changed still more, and so on until they became new horselike animals that lived on after eohippus died out.

This sort of thing happened often during the next 40 million years. It produced larger and larger animals whose backs became straight, not arched. Legs also grew longer and stronger, but some toes became smaller and smaller until they disappeared. At last each foot had only one toe, which formed a large part of the leg and ended in a hoof.

While these things were happening, members of the horse family spread into other parts of the world. Some went southward to the Isthmus of Panama, where they crossed into South America. Other kinds ranged through Canada and Alaska, which in those days was connected with Siberia. This connection allowed the animals to cross into Asia, and then they went to Africa and Europe. In time, herds of true horses roamed across every continent except Antarctica and Australia.

By "true horses" we mean one-toed animals shaped like the horses we know today. But these animals did not look alike. Some grew very tall, but others were less than three feet high. Many kinds were brown, tan, or gray, but those now called zebras developed stripes. One group, whose ears grew long, became the animals we now call asses or donkeys.

At last something new happened — something no one really understands. Although horses, zebras, and asses kept on living in the Old World, their relatives died out in North and South America. So far as we know, the last native horses vanished about 8,000 years ago. America remained horseless until domestic animals were brought from Europe.

Horses were domesticated at least 4,500 years ago, on grassy plains of eastern Europe or western Asia. There, farmers who polished stone tools and weapons tamed animals that looked like the one which Runner and his brother hunted. These Celtic horses had sturdy bodies, short legs, and wide faces. Their manes were short, like the mane of a zebra, but shaggy hair covered their bodies during the winter. Stone-age artists sometimes drew pictures of these horses in their shaggy winter coats. Other pictures show the animals in their short summer hair.

Once farmers discovered that horses were useful, many people began to tame them. Within a few hundred years, horses became the most valued possession of warlike tribes often called Aryans. These people wandered across grassy plains, herding sheep, goats, and cattle, and fighting with other tribes that tried to use their pastures. Since their horses were too small to be ridden far, the Aryans hitched the animals to two-wheeled carts or chariots. The first war chariots were small and were pulled by two horses. Later chariots were larger and were drawn by four horses yoked to a pole, or tongue.

While Aryan tribes were roaming and fighting, people called Sumerians tamed the kiang. This slender horse has such long ears that it resembles an ass. The Sumerians, who lived near the Persian Gulf, hitched domestic kiangs to chariots. But the animals did not become popular, and rich Sumerians began to buy horses of the Celtic type. Domestic kiangs died out, though wild ones still live in southwestern Asia.

Domestic horses remained small for hundreds of years. Then a large breed was developed by the Assyrians, who lived north of Sumer. Soon the Assyrian army had troops of cavalry as well

The kiang is a small, long-eared horse that was domesticated in ancient Sumer.

as war chariots drawn by these new, large horses. Carvings on monuments show Assyrians on horseback hunting lions or spearing them from war chariots.

Horses were first taken to Egypt about 1,700 years before Jesus was born. The animals soon spread through northern Africa, for the Egyptians collected a yearly tribute of horses from the people of Libya. Egyptians also began to sell horses at high prices to kings of small nations in Asia Minor. About 2,900 years ago, King Solomon of Israel bought horses from Egypt, and chariots from Egypt and Syria. One fine chariot cost 600 shekels, but the price of a horse was 150 shekels of silver. At the modern price for silver, this would be about $120. Since money bought much more in ancient times than it does now, the price really was a great deal higher than $120.

War chariots were used by both Greek and Roman armies, and chariots also were driven in races. Mounted horsemen took part in the Olympic games as early as 650 B.C. But the Greeks did not use horses as work animals. More than 2,000 years would go by before horses would become so common that they could be used to pull plows or wagons.

. . .

As domestic horses spread through Asia, Europe, and northern Africa, they mated with other varieties and even species. Ancient Greek horses, for example, seem to have been mixtures of the domesticated Celtic horse and the tarpan. Tarpans are gray or brownish animals that once lived in eastern Russia and central Asia, but now can be seen only in zoos.

About 1,600 years ago, warlike tribes from central Asia began

43

to ride into Europe on horses that also were partly tarpan. These animals were bony and rough-haired, with small heads, straight backs, and sturdy legs. They did not need very good care and could travel 60 miles in a day.

Cavalry horses used by the Romans were mixtures of another type. Almost 3,000 years ago, hunters and farmers in central Europe began to domesticate strong, thick-bodied "forest" horses. Roman conquerors took some of these animals to Italy and mated them with smaller, swifter horses from Africa and Asia Minor. This produced a type that was faster than the forest horse but was big enough to carry a soldier with spear, shield, and armor. Cavalry horses of this type are seen in the sculptures on Roman monuments and temples.

During the first six centuries after Jesus was born, horses became important in Arabia. This is a barren, sandy land where water and feed are scarce and the weather becomes very hot. Ancient Arabs selected horses that could live under such conditions, took good care of them, and bred them to get still better colts. In time, Arabian horses became tall, slender animals that were nervous, hardy, and very swift runners.

When Arabs conquered northern Africa, their horses mixed with others called barbs. Ancient barbs also were fast, slender horses, but they were larger than the Arabian breed and had longer bodies. Barbs also lacked the narrow muzzle and bulging forehead which make Arabian horses look "dish-faced."

Stories about knights in the Middle Ages always describe their "Great Horses." These large, slow, and powerful animals were developed from breeds related to the ancient forest horses. A knight's Great Horse stood more than five feet four inches

44

high at the shoulder, and was ridden by a man whose steel armor covered him from head to foot. During battle the horse wore armor, too, and often it was decorated with velvet robes. Only a big, strong animal could carry such a load.

When armored knights gave way to light cavalry, Great Horses became work animals. At first they pulled carriages and the massive, carved coaches in which noblemen rode. Horses still were too scarce and too costly for ordinary work, which was done by oxen. But in time the Great Horses were used to pull heavy wagons, while teams of lighter, faster horses were hitched to public stage coaches. Still later, descendants of Great Horses were used for plowing, hauling, and other work that had been done by oxen. Though horses were not as strong as oxen, they moved much more rapidly.

.   .   .

As horses became more and more common, many different breeds were developed. All these breeds, however, may be divided among three general groups called draft horses, light horses, and ponies. The first group is further divided into heavy draft and light (or small) draft breeds.

Although we measure most heights in feet, the heights of horses are given in "hands." A hand is equal to four inches, which means that a horse which stands five feet four inches high at the shoulders (called withers) measures just 16 hands. If the animal is five feet three inches high, it is 15.3 hands, or 15 hands and three inches. The figure after a period means inches, not tenths of a hand.

Heavy draft breeds are the world's largest horses, for they are

45

16 to 17.2 hands high and weigh 1,750 to 2,200 pounds. Most of the breeds are descendants of the Great Horses ridden by knights of northern and western Europe. The largest breed of all is the Shire, which was developed in England. The Percheron, which is smaller, came from France, and the Clydesdale was first bred in Scotland. Percherons are often dappled gray, but Clydesdales and Shires may be bay, brown, or even black with white markings. The legs have "feathers" of long hair that make the animals look even larger than they really are.

Light draft horses are 15.3 to 16 hands in height and weigh

The Clydesdale, a heavy draft horse, was developed in Scotland.

1,600 to 1,750 pounds. These are the "general purpose" horses still seen on many farms. One breed, the Canadian, was developed in eastern Canada during the 1700's. It generally is black with a white face.

Light horses may be stocky and plump or tall and very slender. Most breeds are 15 to 16 hands high and weigh 900 to 1,250 pounds. Some light breeds, such as the American Saddle Horse and Thoroughbred, were developed for riding. Others were bred to pull carriages or for "harness" racing. Still other breeds were used either as saddle horses or in harness. In the days before automobiles, these animals pulled the "hacks" that were used instead of taxis.

The Thoroughbred is the slimmest and swiftest of saddle horses; a Thoroughbred once ran a mile in less than one minute

The Canadian is a light draft horse. It was developed during the 1700's.

and 34 seconds. The breed was developed in England and Ireland from Arabian and other ancestors, but Thoroughbreds are now taller and heavier than Arabians. A Thoroughbred in racing condition is 15.1 to 17 hands high but weighs only 900 to 1,150 pounds.

The American Saddle Horse was developed in the South when most roads were too poor for carriages. The breed averages 15.2 hands in height and weighs about 1,100 pounds. The Quarter Horse is another southern breed. It was first developed for racing on tracks one fourth of a mile long. Today this breed is popular on cattle ranches of the Southwest, where it makes a fine "cow pony."

Most harness racers belong to the breed called Standardbred. Many of these horses pace, which means that they move both legs on one side at the same time. Trotters move the foreleg on one side and the hind leg on the other. A horse named Dan Patch was the world's most famous pacer, though one called Billy Direct was a little faster. Trotting horses are not quite so speedy as their pacing relatives, but they are more popular.

Morgan horses once were famous trotters and carriage animals, but they also were sturdy cavalry horses. During the Civil War, General Sherman rode a Morgan, and so did many a less famous soldier. Today Morgans are mostly saddle horses 14.2 to 15.2 hands high and 1,000 to 1,200 pounds in weight. Like Quarter Horses, they are popular "cow ponies."

The palomino is not one breed of horse, but is a color type found in several breeds. The animals have golden-brown bodies but very light manes and tails. Some palominos are bred for ranch work; they are sturdy animals built rather like Quarter

Horses. Other palominos are bred for pleasure riding or for shows and parades. These "show" horses generally are partly Thoroughbred or Arabian, but are heavier than those breeds.

Three breeds of pony are popular in both Europe and North America. The commonest of these is the Shetland, which has lived on the islands north of Scotland since ancient times. Shetland ponies are stocky animals which generally range from 9.3 to 11.2 hands high, though some seen in circuses may be less than five hands. Most of the animals look like tiny draft horses with thick bodies, sturdy legs, and strong muscles. They can live on almost nothing but hay, and those that eat much grain soon become too fat.

The Thoroughbred is a small, slender horse developed for racing.

In Scotland these ponies pull small carts or carry heavy loads on their backs. In America they are ridden or driven by children and in circuses. They also are trained to do tricks, which seem all the more clever if the ponies are very small.

Hackney ponies are small relatives of animals which were bred in England as riding and carriage horses. Hackney ponies are 14.2 hands or less in height, but never are as small as Shetland ponies.

Welsh ponies are descended from small horses that once ran wild among the mountains of Wales. The animals are now 10 to 12 hands in height and make good saddle or driving ponies for older boys and girls. They are not so plump and heavily built as typical Shetland ponies.

.   .   .

We have said that native American horses died out about 8,000 years ago. After that, the New World was horseless until explorers and settlers from Europe brought the animals in ships.

Domestic horses were brought to Mexico by Spaniards in 1519. The Spanish horses belonged to a rather small breed characterized by a broad chest, short neck and legs, and thick body. Colors ranged from dark brown to bay, though some animals were spotted, or "pinto."

Spaniards brought many more horses to Mexico and rode some of them on exploring expeditions to what is now the United States. Many stories say that some of those horses ran wild, or became feral, and then were caught and tamed by Indians. Actually, Indians stole horses from missions and ranches or got the animals from traders. The real feral, or "wild," horses were animals that escaped from the missions and early ranches, and from herds owned by Indians. Spaniards called these animals *mesteños* (meh sten' yoze), or "strayed ones" — horses that belonged to nobody. In time, frontiersmen who could not pronounce Spanish turned the word into "mustang." When ranchmen began to catch mustangs and train them, or "break" them for riding, the word came to mean "cow ponies" of the wild or Spanish type. Though many of these animals were pintos, others were bay, black, white, or buckskin yellow.

These were the early mustangs, before 1850. Early horses in the Southeast also resembled the animals of Spain, for Spaniards settled in Florida during the 1500's. But people who came to the northern Atlantic Coast brought horses from England and other parts of northwestern Europe. When these horses were taken to the West, some of them mated with mustangs. In this way the feral animals changed, becoming more and more like "ordinary" saddle horses and less like those from Spain.

While these things were happening, Indian horses also changed. At first they were Spanish animals, or mustangs, but they mixed with every other breed that the warriors could steal or capture. Since most Indians had not learned how to breed high-grade animals, they rode their best male horses, or stallions, and let the poor ones mate with the mares. In time this produced a variety of small animals, or "ponies," that came to be called cayuses (ky yuse' ez) after one special tribe. Cayuses were hardy but not very strong, and they could not travel nearly as fast as Morgans or American Saddle Horses. The Nez Percé Indians of the Pacific Northwest, however, developed a swift buffalo (bison) runner and war horse. This horse, a paint or pinto,

51

had small brown or black spots usually over the rump. The breed known as the Appaloosa, is a popular saddle horse today.

For many years, horses did most of the hauling and heavy farm work in North America. By 1918 there were about 30 million horses on farms in the United States and Canada. Many more were kept in cities and towns, where they hauled milk wagons and drays, were hitched to buggies, or were ridden for pleasure. Then automobiles, trucks, and tractors became popular, and horses began to disappear. By 1947 there were only 16 million farm horses, and few work horses in cities. You can tell there are still fewer today, for we seldom see city horses except in riding clubs and parks.

Donkeys, Burros, and Mules

IF YOU were to look at a donkey's bones you might not be able to tell them from the skeleton of a pony. But in life the two animals look quite different. Donkeys have long ears and short hair in the mane and tail. The body is deep, the legs are slender, and the hoofs are small. Donkeys also bray loudly with a sound we often call "hee-haw." Actually, the bray starts with a squeaky squeal that is followed by a hoarse roar. These two sounds may be repeated over and over again.

Domestic donkeys are often called asses, for they are descended from the Nubian and perhaps the Somaliland wild ass of northern Africa. The Nubian is a light gray animal 13 to 14 hands in height, with a black stripe down the back and another on each shoulder. The Somaliland ass resembles the Nubian but has dark stripes that run partway around the legs.

Wild asses live on stony hills and deserts. Four or five animals wander about together, feeding during the day but going to drink at night. They are shy and alert, and run swiftly when they are alarmed. Hunters of the Sudan sometimes kill wild asses for meat.

Asses were domesticated in Egypt more than 4,300 years ago. From Egypt they spread through Asia and northern Africa, and into southern Europe. The largest breeds were used for riding, but even they were so small that people had to sit on the animals' haunches. Smaller donkeys were hitched to plows and other implements, or carried loads upon their backs. In ancient Rome, asses often turned mills that ground grain.

At first, all domestic asses were gray, like their wild ancestors. But in time, the large asses developed for riding became black, white, or the pale tan called buckskin. These colors then became common among small work donkeys, for the animals often interbred. But many small asses still have gray coats with black stripes, like their wild ancestors.

In east Africa two new animals — zorses and zebroids — have

African wild asses such as this one were the ancestors of donkeys and burros.

been developed recently. The zorses, produced on a farm in Rhodesia by crossing wild zebra mares and an Arab stallion, have gray coats and faint black stripes on shoulders, hindquarters, and forelegs. The coloring reminds one of the zebra mothers, but the general form of the animals is more like a horse than a zebra. The zebroid, raised in nearby Kenya, is a cross between a donkey and a zebra. The young are used as pack animals.

Donkeys were taken to England and Ireland, though they never became popular in the cool, damp countries of northern Europe. They did best in dry, warm regions such as Italy and Spain. Spaniards brought both large and small asses to Mexico during the early 1500's, and then took them to what is now the southwestern United States. Large asses were — and are — ridden. Small ones, called burros, are the commonest work animals in Mexico and are plentiful as far north as Colorado. Before Jeeps were invented, prospectors loaded their tools and supplies on burros when they went to look for ore.

Burros often escaped from their owners, just as horses did, and joined feral herds. These "wild" asses may be seen in many parts of Mexico and the Southwest. In fact, today more than 10,000 of these descendants of the pack animals roam free in Western United States. They are protected by law as historical symbols on most federal lands except national parks and monuments.

. . .

More than 4,000 years ago, warlike tribes left the deserts near Arabia and invaded thickly settled country near the Persian Gulf. The people traveled on foot, but donkeys carried the baggage. As the tribes captured horses, some of these animals mated with donkeys and produced the world's first mules.

55

We really should say that mules were born when male donkeys, or jacks, mated with female horses, or mares. When a male horse mates with a female donkey, the pair produces a young one called a hinny, which is not very useful. Mules are much more valuable. A good mule combines the large size and much of the strength of a horse with the donkey's sturdiness and resistance to disease. Mules also are more sure-footed than horses and are not so easily frightened. This makes them safer for riding and as pack animals on narrow mountain trails. Still, the animals have two serious faults. First, mules are often as stubborn as any donkey and kick when they become angry. Second, mules almost never have young ones. The only way to get young mules is to mate jacks with mares.

Mules appeared in southwestern Asia soon after horses became common, and then they were bred in Europe. Greek armies had mules as well as horses about 3,200 years ago. The horses were hitched to war chariots, but mules carried loads on their backs. In later times, mules became important riding and work animals. They carried loads and turned mills that ground grain. Caravans of mules carried both riders and baggage. Some people rode astride, on blankets or saddles. Others sat in covered chairs attached to two long poles. The ends of the poles were fastened to the harness of two mules, one in front and one behind. Mules still carry most riders and loads on trails among the mountains of Spain.

.   .   .

We know that asses or donkeys were brought to North America from Europe. Burros are still very much like their Old

World relatives, including the wild asses of North Africa. But the purebred American ass of today was developed by combining five different breeds from Europe. It is a big, strong animal that sometimes weighs 1,000 pounds and is used in breeding mules.

Mules became important work animals during colonial times, especially in the South. Plantation owners of Virginia became especially interested in mules when George Washington began to breed them. The King of Spain sent Washington two fine black asses from the Pyrenees Mountains in 1785, and the Marquis de Lafayette gave him a small ass from Malta. Washington used these animals in his experiments.

Since Washington's time, American breeders have developed mules of several types. By mating asses with large mares, they have produced mules as tall as many horses. By using very small mares, they have bred the little "cotton" mule, which is not much larger than a Great Dane dog.

During the 1800's, Mexican breeders produced small, sturdy mules by mating burros with mustang mares. Many of these mules were sold in the southwestern United States. There the animals pulled carts in mines and carried loads over mountain trails. Teams of 12 to 20 mules also pulled big freight wagons across deserts of the Southwest.

At one time there were almost six million mules on American farms. Their number has become much less since tractors and trucks became common. But many cotton and tobacco farmers still use mules to cultivate their fields.

Cattle, Old and New

APIS walked across the yard of his temple. He paused to eat some hay and grain. Then he lay down in the shade of a wall and lazily chewed his cud.

Apis lived in a temple because he was the sacred bull of Egypt. Priests had found him, when the old sacred bull died, by searching through herds of cattle on farms near the River Nile. They knew Apis when they saw him because he was black with a white triangle on his forehead and a mark shaped like an eagle on his back. He also had a double hair in his tail and a beetle-shaped growth under his tongue. The priests said this growth proved that Apis was a sacred bull.

The priests gave a reward to the man who owned Apis. Then they took the bull to his temple near the city of Memphis. There attendants bathed him regularly and provided him with food. Apis also drank water from his own special spring. The priests said that dirty water from the river was not good enough for such a special bull.

Apis would be the sacred bull for 25 years unless he died before that time. After death he would be made into a mummy and buried in a tomb. Modern scientists who study ancient Egypt have found 35 mummies in the tomb of the sacred bulls.

A Stone-age picture of a bull aurochs following a cow.

Of course, Apis was sacred only to the ancient Egyptians, who worshiped many animals. Apis really was an ordinary bull with some peculiar markings. Like all cattle, he had two large hoof-covered toes on each foot, and two very small ones. He also had two hollow, pointed horns that stayed on his head until he died. Finally, he had a stomach with four parts. When Apis ate grass he swallowed it quickly, letting it go into the first part of his stomach, or rumen (roo' men). Later, when he was not eating, he forced the grass back into his mouth and chewed it thoroughly. Sheep, goats, and antelopes also can do this. We say that all these creatures chew their cuds, or are ruminants (roo' mi nants).

. . .

Wild cattle lived in both Europe and Asia long before Apis became a sacred bull. More than 15,000 years ago, Stone-age hunters drew pictures of cattle on the walls of caves. Many of these pictures show an animal called the aurochs (aw' rox), which was five to six feet high. It had heavy shoulders, a large head, and long horns that curved forward. Cows and calves were dark red, but full-grown bulls were black.

Other cave pictures show wild cattle whose scientific name means "long-faced." They were smaller than the aurochs, and their horns were not so long. In some pictures the horns bend downward. In other pictures they curve upward like the horns of a modern Brown Swiss or Guernsey.

The aurochs once ranged from the British Isles to Switzerland and eastward into Asia. As years went by, it grew more and more scarce. By 1564 only 40 animals were left, and the last aurochs died in 1627.

Although the aurochs has died out, skeletons and ancient pictures tell us how the animal looked. A Greek cup almost 3,500 years old shows hunters trying to capture the aurochs in a net

A bull aurochs as it looked when alive.

A Stone-age drawing of long-faced cattle, from a Spanish cave.

made of rope. Another cup shows domesticated bulls and cows. One is being driven by a man who has tied a rope to the animal's hind foot.

Assyrians and Babylonians hunted the aurochs (or one of its relatives) from chariots. One sculptured monument shows a wounded bull lying on the ground while a younger one is attacking the hunter in his chariot.

Cattle were domesticated in southeastern Europe at least 8,000 years ago. Stone-age tribes that lived near the Caspian Sea began to raise animals that are sometimes called "Persian" cattle. They really were smaller, shorter-horned relatives of the European aurochs.

These tribes were restless people who did not like to stay in one place. In time they wandered westward, taking their "Persian" cattle as well as sheep and goats. Some tribes went to southern Europe, but others traveled northwestward to the

The zebu, or "Brahman," bull has a hump and a dewlap of skin below the neck.

Baltic Sea. Still others wandered into central Europe, where some tribes became Lake Dwellers. They settled in what is now Switzerland about 5,000 years ago.

Bones of two kinds of domestic cattle have been found among ruined lake dwellings. One kind is the lightly built "Persian" cattle that had been brought from Asia. The other is the native aurochs. Perhaps the Lake Dwellers domesticated these big animals. Perhaps wild aurochs bulls mated with short-horned "Persian" cows, producing young ones whose bones cannot be distinguished from those of the European aurochs.

We cannot say which of these things happened. But we are sure that cattle which had been brought from Asia mixed, or interbred, with native species. In eastern Europe this mixture produced animals that became more and more like the big aurochs. In western Europe, cattle began to look like the "long-faced" animals whose pictures are found in caves.

While "Persian" cattle were being driven into Europe, another species was domesticated somewhere in southern Asia. We often call these animals Brahman cattle. Zebus is a better name, for the Brahman is only one breed of zebu.

Zebus are easily recognized by the fleshy humps above their shoulders. A fold of skin, called the dewlap, hangs from the underside of the neck. The horns, which are almost straight, grow upward. The hair ranges from white to light gray or brown, but the skin is dark and the hoofs are black. The animals

Ankole cattle have enormous horns. These animals developed in Africa, from zebu ancestors.

can grunt loudly but they do not bellow or moo. They can stand a great deal of heat as well as weather that is either very damp or very dry.

Zebus were taken to Egypt about 6,000 years ago. There, one breed lost its horns and became spotted. The horns of other types grew longer, but their humps almost disappeared.

From Egypt, humped cattle spread to eastern, southern, and western Africa. One breed, the Afrikander, became big red animals with down-curved horns. Ankole (an ko´ le) cattle developed enormous horns that curve upward and even turn toward one another instead of spreading. Other big-horned cattle reached western Africa and were taken to Spain. There the animals interbred with cattle that already were a mixture of "Persian" and "long-faced" types. Spanish cattle probably got their big horns from their African ancestors.

The water buffalo is an important work animal in warm countries.

The long-haired yak was domesticated in central Asia.

Chinese farmers began to raise cattle at least 4,000 years ago. Some modern Chinese cattle have humps, but others may be distantly related to the ancient "Persian" cattle. Still others are water buffaloes, which like to rest in ponds and streams. They have long wrinkled horns and dark skins that become almost hairless as the animals grow old.

Herds of wild water buffaloes still live in India, where the animals were domesticated at least 2,200 years ago. They have spread through southeastern Asia to the Philippine Islands and Japan. They pull carts, turn mills, and drag logs from forests, but they are most useful in pulling plows through wet, swampy rice fields. In modern times the animals were taken to Egypt and Europe. Many water buffaloes work in the marshes of Hungary, northern Italy, and Spain.

Yaks also have been domesticated for more than 2,000 years.

65

They are shaggy animals with horns that curve upward and skirts of long hair that hang down from their sides. Wild yaks live among the mountains and high plains of Tibet, but domestic varieties are found also in northern India and nearby parts of China and in Mongolia. The animals are ridden, pull carts, or carry loads in high, cold regions where horses and ordinary cattle find life difficult. People also use the milk, meat, and hides of yaks, and make coarse cloth from the hair.

Yaks are often mated with "yellow cattle" of China, which are related to zebus. The hybrid animals are larger than the pure domestic yaks and carry heavier loads. The hybrids also give more milk than yaks and provide better meat.

. . .

Yaks and water buffaloes still are important work animals. Long ago, when horses were scarce and expensive, cattle did most of the hard work on farms. Egyptian paintings and sculptures show oxen hitched to plows, carts, and clumsy sleds that were dragged over the ground. In another ancient carving, a princess rides in a chariot pulled by two hornless, spotted zebus. In northern India, a long-legged type of zebu was bred to carry loads on its back and pull carriages or carts. This long-legged breed also was saddled and ridden, though it could not travel as fast as horses.

Cattle kept on doing work long after horses became common. Oxen were able to drag plows through "heavy" soil or pull wagons over rough, muddy roads. Early settlers in North America used oxen for most of their farm work, and pioneers who settled the West hitched ox teams to their big covered wagons. Oxen also hauled logs that had been cut for lumber.

Modern cowboys often rope steers or wrestle with them in "roundups" and rodeos. Four thousand years ago, on the island of Crete, bull-grappling was a national sport. A man or girl stood in an arena and seized a charging bull by its horns. When the bull tossed its head, the athlete turned a somersault and came down feet-first on the animal's back. Then the athlete leaped to the ground behind the bull.

In time this sport spread to Greece and Rome, and to countries which Rome had conquered. Bull-fighting also began in Rome, though it became most popular in Spain after the year 1040. The English preferred bull-baiting. In this sport a bull was tied to a stake or ran loose in a fenced ring. Specially bred dogs with short muzzles, called bulldogs, seized the bull by the nose or throat. When a dog could not be shaken off, it was declared the victor.

Cattle have been used for meat since very ancient times. At

Head of a southwestern Longhorn.
Some Longhorns still live
in Texas and Oklahoma.

first hunters killed wild animals, and then domestic cattle were butchered. People began to drink milk or make butter and cheese from it. We use milk for ice cream, and we tan hides for leather. Most of our shoes are made of cowhide or calfskin, though other leathers also are used.

As cattle became more and more important, various types and breeds were developed. During the 1700's there were six types of cattle in the British Isles, one of which had come from France. Soon after 1760, several British farmers began to improve both milk and meat cattle by selective breeding. These men mated the best cattle they could find and then bred their best offspring. This produced animals that passed their own good qualities on to their calves.

In time, official "herd books" were started, to register these improved cattle as purebreds. The first herd book registered purebred Shorthorns, which gave large amounts of milk and meat. One famous Shorthorn bull weighed 3,780 pounds.

· · ·

Columbus brought calves from Spain to America in 1493. Later, explorers and settlers took long-horned Spanish cattle to Mexico and South America. In time, the Mexican cattle became the famous Longhorns, which were common in the western United States during early cowboy days. These animals had upward-curving horns five to seven feet wide. They were never milked, and they did not produce very good meat. Later, they were replaced by beef-type Shorthorns from England, and Longhorns almost disappeared. A few still live in Texas and in Oklahoma.

Although we say that Columbus discovered America, he was not the first European to visit our continent. Old stories tell us that Eric the Red, of Norway, took settlers to Greenland before the year 986. These settlers brought cattle as well as horses, sheep, goats, pigs, and dogs. In 1004 another group of Norse settlers took cattle, sheep, goats, and horses to Vinland, in eastern Canada or New England. These were the first domestic animals on the mainland of North America.

In time these Norse settlements were abandoned and their animals disappeared. But cattle of Portuguese, French, and British settlers were cared for and established herds. Although the first animals were poor, better stock was brought soon after it was developed in Europe. The first improved cattle came to

The Guernsey cow gives large amounts of rich milk.

A Hereford bull. This is a famous beef-producing breed.

Virginia, but within a few years shipments were made to other colonies in what now is the United States.

Modern American breeds of cattle are divided among three types: dairy, dual-purpose, and beef. The Holstein-Friesian is our most popular dairy breed. Holstein-Friesians are large black-and-white cattle that originally came from Holland. The cows give a great deal of milk without much cream.

The Jersey, our second most popular dairy breed, gives the richest, or creamiest, milk. Jersey cattle came from an island in the English Channel, near France. Both cows and bulls are small, with "dished" faces and small horns. Colors are tan, tan and white, brownish gray, or almost black.

The Guernsey breed came from an island near Jersey. These

tan-and-white cattle are larger than Jerseys, and their milk contains less cream. Other popular dairy breeds are Brown Swiss, Ayrshire, Dutch Belted, and Canadian. Canadian cattle are hardy brown animals developed from cattle which French settlers brought to Quebec early in the 1600's.

Dual-purpose cattle produce both milk and beef. Most popular are the Shorthorns, which are red, red-and-white, or roan. Beef Shorthorns are big animals that grow rapidly and have shorter legs than milking Shorthorns. Shorthorns replaced Longhorns on the Great Plains, but the breed is now most popular in the north-central part of the United States.

Herefords (hur′ferds) have become our most popular beef cattle. They are big red-and-white animals with white faces and horns that curve downward and forward. They have replaced Shorthorns throughout much of the West. Herefords also are

An Afrikander bull, used to improve southern cattle.

A Santa Gertrudis bull. This modern American breed, which was developed in Texas, is part zebu and part Shorthorn. Its color is very dark red.

seen in other regions, especially where farmers buy western cattle and feed, or "finish," them for market.

The Aberdeen Angus is a hornless, usually coal-black breed smaller than the Hereford. These square-looking animals are popular beef cattle of the East and Southeast. Crossed with Holsteins, they yield high milk and good beef.

Crossing especially with foreign breeds, many of them imported by way of Canada, such as the Simmental and the cream-colored Charolais, a well-known beef animal, is becoming common. The Simmental, long a major European breed, is rather new in the Americas. It is buff or dull red and white and is bigger than the Angus or the Hereford. Already American cattlemen are finding it makes a fine all-purpose animal, good for meat, draft, and milk.

Breeds of cattle that were first developed in Europe often suffer from heat and insect pests in low, hot regions near the Gulf of Mexico. But zebus are native to hot countries of Asia where insects and diseases are common. Afrikanders also live well in similar parts of southern Africa.

Scientists, farmers, and ranchmen want to combine the sturdiness of zebus and Afrikanders with the beef qualities of European breeds. Zebus were brought to the United States in 1849, and Afrikanders were taken to Texas in 1931. Various crosses have been made with Herefords and Shorthorns. The most successful of these is the Santa Gertrudis breed, developed on the great King Ranch in Texas. Santa Gertrudis cattle are big, powerful animals that are three-eighths zebu and five eighths Shorthorn. They have almost no hump above their shoulders and their coats are dark red, but the dewlap that hangs from the throat shows they are related to zebus. The animals fatten well and make fine beef.

Crosses of Afrikander-Herefords and Afrikander-Shorthorns have been developed on both the King and the Kenedy ranches in Texas. Some of these animals are now living in semidesert regions. Others are doing well in Florida, where the climate is moist as well as hot, and pastures are often poor.

A different experiment has been made in Canada. There, scientists have crossed yaks with European cattle to develop breeds that can live on the cold plains and in the northern forests.

Wild Boars, Hogs, and Hot Dogs

"OINK, OINK!" grunted Porky, a fat white pig. Then he began to root among the alfalfa plants that grew in the field where he lived. Porky pushed his flat nose into the ground, grubbed out an earthworm, and ate it. Then he munched a green plant. He would eat almost anything, from earthworms to growing plants and dry grain.

The white pig was only six months old, but he weighed 200 pounds. In a few weeks he would "put on" 30 or 40 pounds more. When he did that, he would be called a hog, not a pig. He also would be ready to be marketed and made into meat.

Porky was not a pet like most cats and dogs. He and other pigs did not give milk, as cows do, and he did not work like horses and oxen. His only job was to eat and grow, so the farmer could sell him. If the pig grew rapidly, the farmer would make a profit when Porky was sold.

People often think that pigs and grown-up hogs are stupid, dirty creatures. But scientists have found that these animals really are more intelligent than cattle or horses. The pig seems to be stupid because he has short legs, a big awkward body, and a thick head. Besides, people seldom train him to work or teach him tricks, as they teach horses.

Pigs are clean unless people keep them in dirty places. The farmer who owned Porky gave him a clean, dry pasture and put his food on a concrete platform. There also was a pool of cool, clean water. Porky bathed in the pool on very hot days, for his skin had no sweat glands to cool his body. Porky was healthier and grew much faster than pigs kept in dirty pens.

We have seen that wild horses once were native to North America. So are the hump-backed wild cattle often called buffaloes, though their proper name is bison. But real pigs, or swine, lived only in Asia, Africa, and Europe until human beings took them to other parts of the world. Native American wild "pigs" are peccaries. Although they grunt and root for food, they belong to their own family.

Wild boars once ranged from the British Isles to southwestern Asia and northern Africa. They are shaggy gray animals that sometimes grow more than three feet high and weigh 250 to 300 pounds. They have long tusks on their lower jaws and can fight fiercely when they are attacked. People now hunt boars for sport, but Stone-age hunters killed them for meat and sometimes painted their pictures in caves. One painting shows a running boar. To make it seem to go fast, the Stone-age hunter painted eight legs instead of four.

Swine were domesticated at about the same time as sheep, goats, and cattle. We think that people began by taming pigs of a variety of wild boar that still lives in the forests of southern Asia. The little pigs made cute pets, and women and children took care of them.

As years went by, these hunter-farmers wandered away from their homes. Some of them went northward to China. Some went eastward to islands in the Pacific Ocean. Others went westward through Asia to Africa and Europe. No matter where they went, these people took their pigs and other livestock. Perhaps children herded the pigs or drove them with leather ropes tied to the beasts' hind legs.

We do not know just when domestic pigs were first taken out of the forests of Asia. But farmers who lived in Iraq 7,000 years ago raised pigs and ate their meat. Bones of pigs have been found in the ruins of early Egyptian towns and near Lake-dweller villages that were built about 5,000 years ago. Chinese farmers were raising pigs 4,000 to 5,000 years ago.

Swine, like cats and cattle, became sacred animals. Clay pigs have been found in ancient Egyptian graves. Sumerians sacrificed swine to their gods and ate pork at religious banquets. The Greeks sacrificed pigs to their goddess of grain. When the Ro-

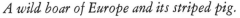

A wild boar of Europe and its striped pig.

mans made a treaty with some other nation or with a tribe, a priest killed a pig with a sacred stone knife.

But pigs were not always sacred. There were times when Egyptians thought pigs were "unclean" and would not let swineherds enter temples. The Israelites did not eat pork. In Scotland the Devil was called a "big black pig," and the Scot who became King James I of England "loved no part of a swine."

. . .

Wild boars are forest animals, and ancient domestic pigs ran loose in woodlands, where they mated with wild animals. Domestic pigs of the Lake Dwellers and other early Europeans interbred with the wild boar. Other crosses with wild pigs probably took place in the forests of eastern Asia.

Norsemen brought swine to America, but the animals died. Columbus brought eight young pigs on his second voyage, in 1493. In the early 1500's Spanish conquerors took pigs to Florida and Mexico, and then to New Mexico. Spanish pigs were captured or stolen by Indians. Instead of raising the animals, the Indians let them run wild in the forest and then hunted them. The Indians were not used to raising and feeding animals that could take care of themselves.

English colonists who came to Virginia in 1607 also brought domestic pigs. At first the animals ran loose in the forests, eating acorns and other food. Later, as plantations spread, rail fences were built to keep the animals at home. But many hogs squeezed through the fences and escaped. They joined the descendants of hogs turned loose in earlier times, forming a feral race known as razorbacks. Razorbacks are slim animals with

The Hampshire, developed in Kentucky, is a lard-type breed.

long legs, tusklike teeth, and coarse hair. They look and act much like the wild boars of Europe.

Real wild boars were brought from Germany in 1912, and were set free on a hunting preserve among the mountains of North Carolina. Some of the animals escaped and interbred with razorbacks. Wild boars from this hunting preserve were shipped to California in 1924. Some of them also escaped.

Puritans and other colonists in New England also brought swine from England. Many of these animals ranged the woods in herds. Swineherds drove them to and from their feeding grounds and tried to keep the animals from escaping. By the time of the Revolution, in 1776, many New England farmers owned four or five hogs. They were fattened on corn and were sold or butchered to provide families with smoked and salted pork.

Hog raising became a great industry after the Middle West

was settled during the 1800's. Farms in this region produced enormous amounts of clover, grass, and corn, which is the best of all grains for fattening hogs. Farmers began to keep more and more of these animals, butchering a few and selling the rest to packing houses in Cincinnati, Chicago, and other cities. Since Americans could not eat all the pork from so many hogs, much of it was sent to Europe.

Not many years ago, most farmers raised big hogs that produced fat meat as well as large amounts of lard. Then people began to use less lard for cooking and bought lean pork instead of fat. Scientists also discovered that feeding hogs until they grew very big and fat cost too much. When these facts became widely known, farmers began to raise smaller, meatier animals that could be sold when they weighed 200 to 250 pounds. Good farmers also began to feed hogs carefully and keep them in clean pastures, not in dirty, muddy pens.

Hogs raised on American farms today belong to two general groups, called the lard type and the bacon type. Hogs of the lard type have plump bodies and fairly long legs, and their hind quarters (or hams) are as wide as their shoulders. Hogs of the bacon type are longer, taller, and thinner, and their hind quarters are not so wide. Bacon-type hogs are almost the only ones raised in Canada.

Ten different breeds of lard hogs are common on American farms, and eight of them were developed in the United States. The three most popular breeds are Duroc Jersey, Poland China, and Chester White. The Duroc Jersey is a big, hardy, red animal with a rather small head. The Poland China is black with white marks, though a closely related breed is spotted. Chester Whites

79

have long, straight legs, short necks, and arched backs. They were developed by crossing common white hogs of Chester County, Pennsylvania, with animals from England.

The Hampshire is a popular breed because the newborn pigs are large and grow rapidly. Hampshire hogs are black with a white "belt" that goes around the body at the shoulders and extends into the forelegs.

The two imported breeds of lard hogs are the Berkshire and the Large Black. Both were brought from England. Berkshires are black with white marks, or "points," on the face, feet, and tail. They also are the only American hogs with turned-up snouts. The breed was developed by crossing very large British hogs with small ones imported from Asia.

The Large Black breed really grows no bigger than the Chester White. You can tell Large Blacks by their wide, floppy ears, which hang downward and almost cover the eyes. The breed is more popular in Canada than in the United States.

Most Canadian hogs belong to two bacon breeds, the Yorkshire and the Tamworth. Both came from England, and both

The Yorkshire, a bacon-type hog from England, is popular in Canada.

are raised in the United States as well as in Canada. Yorkshires generally are white, though black spots may appear on the skin. Tamworth hogs are red, with long heads and narrow upright ears. The legs are longer than those of most of the other breeds.

When two different breeds of animals are mated, their young ones often show "hybrid vigor." This means that they are stronger or healthier than their parents, or grow larger and faster. Mules are animals that show hybrid vigor, for they grow larger than donkeys and are more hardy than horses.

Both scientists and farmers have discovered that pigs with parents of different breeds may also show hybrid vigor. Several different breeds have been crossed, producing pigs that grow faster than their parents. Other hybrids become lean hogs, which sell for better prices than fat ones. One special breed, the Landrace, was imported from Denmark to develop some of these lean hybrids that are fitted for life on American farms.

.   .   .

There are about 60 million hogs in the United States, and millions more in Canada. They eat almost half of the American corn crop and large amounts of other grains. Hogs also eat soybeans, flax, clover, alfalfa, and feed that contains vitamins as well as ground-up bone.

When hogs become large enough for market, they provide lard, leather, and at least half of our meat. You can see it at the supermarket in the form of hams, calas (shoulders), bacon, chops, loin roasts, and spareribs. Several kinds of sausage are made from pork, or from pork mixed with beef.

Sausage is a popular food, but it is not a new one. Long before the time of Jesus, people chopped pork into small pieces. Then the chopped meat was flavored with salt, pepper, and other spices. The mixture was packed into pigs' intestines which had been washed until they were clean. Sheeps' intestines were used as "casings" for small sausages.

The Chinese may have made the first sausage soon after they began to raise hogs. Ancient Greeks also made sausage, and Romans served it with roasted wild boar. In time, sausages of different kinds were developed in different places. Bologna sausage, for example, was made in the Italian city of Bologna. Wieners were used in Vienna, which the Austrians call Wien. Frankfurters took their name from the German city of Frankfurt, and so on.

The "hot dog" is only a large frankfurter renamed by Americans. In 1883, a man named Anton Feuchtwanger began to sell freshly cooked frankfurters at his lunch stand in St. Louis. At first he provided cotton gloves so his customers would not burn their fingers. Later, he put each frankfurter in a roll that had been cut lengthwise. In 1900 a cartoonist drew some frankfurters sizzling on a grill and labeled the picture "Bow-wow!" Another cartoonist showed a Dachshund falling into a sausage mill. The dog came out with its head, legs, and tail unharmed, but its body had become a string of frankfurters. Soon people began to use the name "hot dog" for this highly flavored kind of sausage, which can be boiled, fried, or broiled.

Camels With and Without Humps

A CARAVAN was crossing the Persian desert in the year 1250. First came the caravan master and several other merchants, riding on horses. They were followed by a long line of camels, each tied to the one in front. Every camel carried boxes or bundles filled with goods which the merchants planned to sell when they reached the city of Baghdad. Drivers with camel sticks walked beside the animals.

The pads of the camels' feet made shuffling sounds in the sand. Again and again the drivers shouted or prodded the beasts to make them go faster. Sometimes the camels grunted, and sometimes they gave bubbling screams. Now and then they twisted their long necks sideways and tried to bite the drivers.

As evening came, the leading camel sniffed and began to hurry. "She smells water!" said the caravan master. "Soon we shall see the village where we can rest for the night."

When the village first appeared, it looked like a dark dot. Then it became a cluster of houses made of sun-baked brick surrounded by a wall. Green date palms made long shadows in the setting sun.

At last the caravan entered the village gate. The drivers loosened ropes and belts, taking boxes, bundles, and pack saddles from the camels' backs. As each camel was unloaded, it was given a drink of water and a few dates to eat. Then one front foot was tied up with a rope, and the animal was turned out to browse on thorny shrubs around the village. No camel could wander far away when it had to hobble on three legs.

. . .

A long time has passed since that particular caravan traveled toward Baghdad. Airplanes now fly to the city, and automobiles travel farther in an hour than caravans can go in a day. Yet caravans still are common, and camels are more plentiful than they were in the year 1250. About 10 million of the long-legged animals pull plows, turn water wheels, or carry loads and riders across the deserts of Africa and Asia.

Still, the first camels were not desert animals, and they did not live in the Old World. The camel family appeared on prairies in the American West only a few million years after dawn horses lived there. And camels kept on living in the West until long after human beings came to North America.

Early members of the camel family were little, humpless animals with four toes on each front foot but only two behind. As ages went by, these small creatures produced young ones that became larger and larger. Their necks became longer, too, and they lost two toes from each forefoot. Some had only hoofs, but others developed pads on the undersides of their toes.

As these new, larger camels developed, they began to wander. Some went to South America, where their descendants became the guanaco (gwa nah' co) and vicuña (vi kyu' nya). Others traveled through western Canada and Alaska and then crossed

The guanaco is a wild South American camel. It has no hump.

a strip of land that ran from North America to Asia. Some of these creatures became modern camels with humps. They spread through Asia to Africa and Europe and perhaps came back to America.

Do you recall that many wild horses died out a few thousand years ago? The same thing happened to camels. First they died out in North America and Europe. Then they became scarce in Africa and most of Asia. At last only four kinds remained, two in South America and two in the Old World.

Camels of South America are humpless and they never grow very large. The guanaco is four feet high at the shoulder. The reddish-brown hair is coarse, and the feet have small pads as well as hoofs. Guanacos are sometimes found among mountains, but they are commonest on plains east of the Andes. There they once ran in herds of 500 to 5,000 animals. The largest herds have disappeared since the country was settled by white men.

Indians domesticated guanacos at least 3,000 years before white men came to South America. In time the domestic animals divided into llamas and alpacas. Llamas became larger than guanacos, with sturdier bodies and longer necks. They also became variable in color. Many llamas are white with yellowish-brown spots, but some are brown or brownish black.

The llama is a domesticated camel used as a pack animal in South America.

The alpaca is a domesticated South American camel that produces wool.

No one knows where llamas were first developed, but Peru and Bolivia became the great centers in which they were bred. The Incas and other ancient Indians kept herds of llamas as pack animals. A large male could carry 100 to 120 pounds on his back and travel about 12 miles a day. The animals also were ridden, but they could not be overloaded. When a llama found his pack too heavy, he lay down and refused to move until it was taken off. The animals also balked when they were tired. If a driver prodded a llama or shouted at it, the beast turned its head and spat in the man's face.

Spaniards brought donkeys and horses to South America, but they also used llamas to carry silver and gold from mines. Llama trains still carry loads in Peru, Bolivia, and northern Chile. The animals travel single file along roads or on steep, narrow trails. Only the males work; the females are kept for milk and meat. When the animals are not being used they are taken to high mountain pastures, where they sometimes mate with wild guanacos. Only one lamb is born at a time. It is a long-legged, woolly little creature that begins to play around its mother soon after it is born.

Llama wool is so coarse that it is used only for cord, rope, and the poorest kinds of cloth. Indians get fine wool from alpacas. These descendants of the guanaco are bred especially for their

The dromedary, of Asia and Africa, has only one hump.

fleeces. Alpacas are smaller than llamas and have shorter legs. They generally are dark brown or black, though they may be light brown, or brown-and-white. Their fleeces consist of long outer wool, which is rather coarse, and underwool that is shorter and finer. The fine wool is dyed, spun, and woven into caps, blankets, and sashes. Blankets called ponchos have holes for the head and are worn instead of coats.

The largest herds of alpacas are found in Bolivia and southern Peru. Attempts to raise alpacas in Australia and other countries have not been successful.

.   .   .

Camels of Asia and Africa belong to two species. One of these species has one hump, but the other has two humps.

The one-humped camel is called the dromedary (drum′ e day ri), though that name is also used for a special breed of riding camel. Dromedaries are big, long-legged animals that grow six to seven feet high at the shoulder. The hair is not very long, and its color ranges from white to black, though light sandy brown is commonest.

There were herds of one-humped camels in western Arabia and northern Egypt about 5,000 years ago. But the animals were wild, for dromedaries probably were not domesticated until about 1,000 years before Jesus was born.

The people who domesticated dromedaries were herdsmen who wandered with their flocks. They found that the camels could carry heavy loads or riders. The females gave milk, and camel meat tasted as good as mutton. The hair made feltlike cloth for tents, and the dried dung was used for fuel.

Dromedaries also were easy to care for. They liked grass, grain, or even dried dates. But they could feed on dry, thorny bushes, which they chewed without hurting their mouths. While food was plentiful the animals ate all they could. Instead of wasting food they did not need, their bodies turned it into fat and stored it in their humps. When food became scarce, the animals used up this fat. A dromedary with a fine big hump could work for several days with only a little food.

Stranger still, the dromedary seemed able to live without water. The animal actually swallowed gallons of water when it could, and when it was very thirsty. Part of this water was stored in pockets of the stomach. Like stored-up fat, the water was used later, when the animal could not get a drink.

In rainy seasons dromedaries fed on juicy plants. At such times, the animals could go for weeks or months without drinking. The moisture in leaves and stems provided all the water they needed for active, hard-working life.

As years passed, wild dromedaries disappeared, but domestic herds became more and more important. Big animals were bred to carry loads of 300 to 600 pounds. Smaller, slender breeds were developed for riding. The animals' padded feet move over loose sand with ease, and their short hoofs do not dig into it. A good riding dromedary can travel seven to nine miles per hour, or 70 to 100 miles in a day.

Work dromedaries are sometimes harnessed to carts, to plows, or to crude mills for grinding grain. This is done most often in Egypt, where dromedaries became popular after Arabs conquered the country about 1,300 years ago. Domesticated dromedaries spread across northern Africa and were taken to Spain,

Italy, and Australia. The United States Army brought camels to Texas in 1856 and used them as pack animals when a road was opened across northern Arizona in 1857.

The dromedaries traveled 25 to 35 miles a day, carrying water for mules that pulled wagons. The camels climbed mountains and ridges, working when mules and horses were exhausted. But soldiers disliked the dromedaries, which were stupid and bad-tempered, and often tried to bite men who rode near them. The camels also frightened horses, and made cattle stampede. In time, some of the dromedaries were sold, and the rest were turned loose on the Arizona desert. A few were recaptured and used to carry ore from mines. The others were finally killed by Indians and by white mule drivers, who hated the dromedaries.

The Bactrian camel, of Asia, has two humps.

Bactrian (bak' tri an) camels get their name from a province in ancient Persia. There the animals probably were domesticated about 3,000 years ago.

The Bactrian camel can be recognized by its two humps, and its legs are shorter than those of the dromedary. Even a large male may be less than five feet high at the shoulder, or six to seven feet at its humps. Colors range from cream to red or light brown. The hair is woolly and long, especially on the neck. The hair is pulled off while the animal is shedding. An average camel produces more than five pounds of hair per year.

When a Bactrian camel is ridden, the rider sits between the humps. Most of the animals carry loads, which generally range from 150 to 600 pounds. A loaded camel walks at an average rate of four miles an hour on short trips and two miles an hour on long ones.

The two-humped animals are hardy and can stand both heat and cold. They have been taken to central Asia, northern China, and southern Siberia, where they travel across hilly country as well as stony deserts. Leather is sometimes sewed over their feet to protect them.

Like wild dromedaries, wild Bactrian camels have disappeared since their relatives were domesticated. Herds that now run wild are feral. Now and then Bactrian camels interbreed with dromedaries. No hybrid breed has been developed because these animals almost never have young ones.

Cats of Many Kinds

WHISKERS, a black house cat, was lying beside a fireplace. The heat made him feel so warm that he purred happily. But soon he stood up and arched his back. Then he walked to the kitchen, waving the tip of his tail.

Whiskers went to a saucer of milk that sat on the kitchen floor. He crouched down in front of the saucer and lapped up the milk with his pink tongue.

When the saucer was empty, Whiskers sat up and began to wash himself. He used his tongue to wipe the milk from his lips and from his long white whiskers. Then he licked both fore-paws and used them as if they were damp washcloths, rubbing his face and the fur around his ears. Finally he ran his tongue over the pads on the undersides of his feet.

As soon as Whiskers finished washing, he went back to the living room. There he stopped beside his mistress and rubbed his sides against her ankles. When she sat down, he jumped into her lap and began to move his forepaws up and down. He did this again and again before snuggling down to rest. Then he shut his black-and-yellow eyes and purred.

After resting awhile, Whiskers hopped down to the floor and walked to the door. There he turned toward his mistress.

The Egyptian wildcat was domesticated about 5,000 years ago.

"Meow meow," he said in a soft voice. After each "meow" he looked up at the door.

The woman knew what Whiskers meant. He wanted her to let him out. When she held the door open, he walked past her and across the porch. At the edge of the porch he paused to look around. Then he went down the steps and into the yard.

When dogs go outdoors they often bark and run about as if they are playing. But Whiskers did not make a sound, and he did not run. He walked to a tree instead, and prowled round the trunk. Then he stood on his hind legs and reached upward as high as he could. Extending the claws on his forefeet, he pulled them downward over the bark. This is a cat's way of sharpening his claws. The rough bark rubbed a scaly layer from them, making the claws smooth and sharp. They were ready to be used in climbing or for catching food.

Whiskers was seldom hungry, but he liked to hunt. He often went out at night, prowling around the yards in his neighborhood. He also liked to hunt in the daytime, when the weather was not too hot.

Soon after Whiskers sharpened his claws, he saw some blades of grass move to and fro. A human being might have said to himself, "That grass is moving against the breeze. There must be a mouse on the ground!" But Whiskers could not talk, to himself or anyone else, and he did not take time to think things out. Instead, he crouched down and began to creep forward. Before the mouse suspected that Whiskers was near, the cat leaped forward and pounced upon it.

Dogs and wolves bite their prey and then hold it, but Whiskers did not bite. He struck the mouse with one paw and then backed away. When the mouse got up and tried to escape, Whiskers struck it again. He did this several times, until the mouse was dead. Then the cat picked it up and carried it to the house. When his mistress opened the door to let him in, he laid the dead mouse at her feet.

.　.　.

Whiskers is a modern cat, and he lives in a modern home. It has electric lights, a furnace, and a refrigerator that cools his milk. When he goes to the "vet," or animal doctor, he rides in an automobile.

Whiskers would not have had these things if he had lived in ancient Egypt. But he would have been safe, happy, and comfortable. In fact, his home might have been much better than the homes of most human beings.

There have been wildcats in Egypt for ages, and one species still lives there. These wild animals have short yellowish-gray fur with dark spots and stripes, and black tips on their tails. The pads of bare skin on the undersides of the feet also are black, and black extends all the way to their heels. Egyptian wildcats look a good deal like house cats, and the animals frequently mate.

Egyptians began to tame wildcats about 5,000 years ago. Fathers probably brought kittens home to their children, for the little animals were playful. Then someone found that grown-up cats were useful, for they caught mice and rats that came to feed in granaries. Hundreds of years later, cats were trained to hunt wild birds that had been shot with arrows. When a hunting cat caught a wounded bird, he took it to his master.

As hundreds of years went by, domestic cats changed color. Some became darker gray than their wild relatives, others became black and white, and some had brown spots. Statues show that these ancient cats had long legs, large ears, and broad faces. Cats of modern Egypt show all these characteristics, as well as big yellow eyes. They also are very friendly and are attractive pets.

Animals that were useful and friendly often became sacred. In Egypt, domestic cats became sacred to a goddess called Bastet. People said Bastet could come to earth whenever she wished, and turn herself into a cat. Because of this, no one was allowed to kill a cat or even to hurt it. There were special cat holidays, and sacred cats were buried in the temple of Bastet. Many statues of the goddess show her with the head of a lion. In other statues Bastet has a cat's head.

Rich Egyptians also kept pet cats in their homes. These animals were treated almost like human beings. They ate fine food, wore gold rings in their ears, and had servants who took care of them. When the animals died they were made into mummies and buried in special cemeteries. One ancient cemetery contained the mummies of 180,000 cats.

Long before Jesus was born, cats were taken from Egypt to western Asia. From there the animals were carried to Greece and Rome, and eastward to China. Books written more than 2,500 years ago tell about cats in wealthy Chinese homes.

The Romans took cats to Britain almost 2,000 years ago. Still, cats were not common in either Rome or ancient Greece. For

At the right is a small statue of the Egyptian goddess, Bastet. She has a cat's head and a basket of kittens.

This figure of a cat once stood upon a cat's coffin.

"mousers" the people kept ferrets, which are related to weasels. Ferrets also came from Africa, but they could not be domesticated like cats. After more than 2,000 years ferrets still are wild animals. They often bite people who own them, and run away unless they are kept in cages.

When cats from Egypt were taken to Europe, they sometimes mated with wildcats that were common in forests. The European wildcat is closely related to the African species, but it is much harder to tame. The European animal also has longer fur and a longer tail. The pads on its feet are pinkish, with only small spots of black. Some domestic cats now have spotted pads, but others still have black pads like those of the wildcats tamed in Egypt.

Europeans became farmers long before cats were brought from Egypt. As years went by, the farmers had more and more trouble with mice that got into granaries and destroyed good food. At last the farmers began to keep cats instead of ferrets,

Two bronze statues of Egyptian cats. One statue was also a cat's coffin.

and these cats became very valuable. More than 1,000 years ago, a Welsh law gave protection to cats that were "guardians of the King's granary." Anyone who killed one of these cats had to pay a fine. This fine was enough wheat to cover the animal when it was hung up by the tail with its nose just touching the floor. Another old law said that anyone who killed a cat had to pay for it with a ewe and a lamb.

Although cats became valuable mouse-killers, they were not kept as pets. In fact, many Europeans became afraid of cats and thought they were evil animals that helped witches or the Devil. Crowds sometimes tortured cats, crucified them, or burned them alive. Many people thought witches could turn themselves into cats and ride through the air to meetings held for the worship of Satan. Although no one believes such things nowadays, we still put black cats with witches in the decorations used at Halloween. We also say, as a joke, that we'll have bad luck if a black cat runs in front of us.

Cats could not become pets until they were kept in houses. But most people of Europe did not want cats in their homes. So cats stayed in barns and sheds until about the year 1300, when rats became common in Europe.

Two kinds of "common" rats live in buildings, and both of them came from Asia. The dark gray, or "black," rat came first, for it wandered from India to Palestine and nearby countries about 1,000 years ago. There it stayed until the Crusades, which were wars in which Christian armies from Europe tried to take the Holy Land away from Mohammedans.

Some Christian armies traveled to Palestine by land, but others went in ships. While the ships were tied up in port, black

The Manx cat (left) has no tail.

The tabby (right) has a long tail and dark marks on its fur.

Two very different domestic cats.

rats went aboard. When the ships sailed home they carried these rats, which then went ashore in Europe. There they spread from seaports to villages, and from one village to another. In a few years, black rats became common in barns, granaries, and houses. People had to keep cats in their homes to kill some of these troublesome rats.

Cats became still more necessary when brown rats arrived. They came by land from central Asia, crossing western China and Russia. The rats reached Germany and France before 1700, and then went to the British Isles on ships. Brown rats began to live in London about 1730.

Although cats were useful ratcatchers, many persons still thought they were evil. At last that idea died out, and people began to keep cats in their houses as pets. By the time brown rats reached England, Europeans had several sorts of house cats. During the 1700's, long-haired cats from Turkey and Persia became popular in Europe. At first the two types were distinguishable, but they have interbred. Today we use the name Persian for almost all long-haired cats.

After 1700, more and more people became "cat fanciers." They kept special breeds of cats and gave prizes for the finest animals. The world's first cat shows were held in Maine, during the 1860's. London's cat shows began in 1871, and the New York shows started in 1895. The United States now has about a hundred cat-breeding societies that hold shows and give prizes for the finest animals. Newspapers often publish pictures of prize-winning cats.

.   .   .

We divide all domestic cats into short-haired and long-haired breeds. Many short-haired cats still look like the wildcats of Europe and northern Africa. This is easy to understand, for "common" short-haired cats almost surely are a mixture of the sacred cat of ancient Egypt and the European wildcat. Long-haired cats, or Persians, probably came from the manul, or Pallas cat, a small wildcat that lives in central Asia. Its long, soft hair is buff or silvery gray with black marks. Many long-haired cats also have crossed with short-haired types and have inherited their colors.

Many people call all mother cats "tabbies." Actually, tabbies are short-haired cats whose fur has one solid color, with barlike marks of a darker shade. Many tabbies are gray and black, but others are brownish-red or silver. Tortoiseshell cats are a mixture of black, red-brown, and cream. Most of them are females, but they are not tabbies.

Manx cats have no tails, though some have tufts of fur where the tails should be. The hind legs are so long that the animals seem to hop when they run. One story says that Manx cats are descended from Oriental cats, some of which have no tails. The animals were supposedly kept on Spanish ships as ratcatchers. They were washed ashore on the Isle of Man, near England, when Spanish vessels were wrecked there in 1588.

Maltese cats are bluish gray and have short hair. They probably are descendants of Russian "blue" cats, which are common in northern countries. These cats did not come from Malta, an island in the Mediterranean Sea.

Siamese cats became popular during modern times. These cats are slender, with long tapering tails that may be slightly kinked near the end. The eyes are blue and are often crossed, and the general color is cream, yellow-brown, chocolate, or pale gray. Ears, legs, feet, tail, and face may be dark brown, gray, or the color of milk chocolate. The original Siamese cats were short-haired, but long-haired types have been developed by crossing these animals with Persians.

Siamese cats probably came from Khorat, in northwestern Siam (now Thailand). The breed entered England in 1884, when the King of Siam gave a pair to the British consul-general in Bangkok. Other people soon obtained some of the cats and began to breed them. We think Siamese cats were first brought to America in 1895. Many people say these animals are more intelligent than any other breed.

Burmese cats are deep chocolate in color. They usually have long hair, too, and their eyes are yellow. In spite of these differences, they may have been developed from the Khorat cat. For hundreds of years, traders from Khorat traveled to Burma to sell silk. The traders probably took cats as well as silk and gave them to rich ladies of Burma. In time, the Khorat cats mated with long-haired, yellow-eyed "Persian" cats, producing the Burmese breed.

Many domestic cats of India are spotted like the native desert cat. This animal is a close relative of the North African wildcat. It sometimes mates with Indian house cats, just as European wildcats mated with domestic cats from Egypt.

Persian and Siamese cats. Although Persians have long hair and are very popular house cats, they readily "run wild," or become feral.

Guinea Pigs, Rabbits, and Hares

TWO full-grown guinea pigs and their five young ones ran about on the dirt floor of a hut. An Indian family sat on the floor, eating from a bowl of soup. The guinea pigs scampered among the people. The animals peered into corners with their dark eyes, and their stubby noses twitched.

The hut in which the Indians and guinea pigs lived was among the Andes Mountains of Peru. The walls were made of stone and dry mud, but the roof was covered, or thatched, with straw. There were no windows and only one door. Smoke from a fire filled the hut and worked its way out through the low doorway.

Although the Indian family was poor, their guinea pigs had plenty to eat. They nibbled grass and tender plants that grew near the hut. Now and then an Indian gave them some corn or peelings from potatoes. With so much food, the young guinea pigs were growing rapidly. In two months they would be sleek and fat, and so large that the Indians would cook them and eat them. By that time, the mother and father guinea pig would be raising another litter of babies. They would not worry about those that had grown up, or wonder where they were.

The guinea pig, which we sometimes call a cavy (kay' vie), is a native of South America. It belongs to the group of creatures

Guinea pigs of the English breed (left) and so-called Peruvian breed (right).

called rodents, or gnawing animals. Squirrels, prairie dogs, mice, and porcupines also are rodents. All these animals have two pairs of chisel-edged teeth at the front of the mouth. These chisel teeth are used for gnawing and cutting, yet they never wear down to short stubs. This is because they keep on growing throughout life, just as your fingernails do.

Wild cavies of several kinds are found in South America. The restless cavy of Brazil and Uruguay is a nervous, fidgety animal that grows to be 10 inches long. It has short legs and almost no tail, and its coarse fur is reddish brown. The Peruvian cavy is smaller, and its soft hair is black or very dark brown. Bolivian cavies are gray-and-white, and so are rock cavies.

Guinea pigs apparently came from Peruvian cavies. These animals were domesticated at least 1,000 years ago, probably by Indians who lived in the region that is now northern Chile. Some guinea pigs still are black or dark brown, but others are white, tan, or spotted. They become almost as long as the restless cavy and often weigh one to one and a half pounds. The animals murmur softly when they are happy, squeal when they are frightened, and grunt when they want food.

105

When white men came to South America, they found guinea pigs in Chile, Bolivia, Peru, Ecuador, and near the Caribbean Sea. Some books say that Spaniards first took the animals to Europe, and others say that Dutch explorers did so. Settlers from Europe then brought guinea pigs to North America. Englishmen probably named the animals "pigs" because they grunt. "Guinea" may come from slave traders, or "guineamen," who brought the animals to England. The name also may come from Guiana, a region in South America beside the Caribbean Sea.

There are three important breeds of guinea pigs, called Peruvian, Abyssinian, and English. The Abyssinian and Peruvian breeds are raised as pets and for shows. The English breed is used in laboratories, for medical experiments or to test serums and antitoxins. The animals have silky hair and make good pets, for they are clean and do not bite.

Wild cavies breed twice a year and have one or two young ones. Domestic guinea pigs breed every 9 or 10 weeks and have 4 to 12 babies. The little ones are born with their eyes open and full coats of fur. They run about soon after their birth and begin to eat leaves, vegetables, and corn when they are two or three days old.

.   .   .

Rabbits and hares were once called rodents, for they have chisel-edged gnawing teeth. But rodents have only two pairs of these teeth, while rabbits and hares have three pairs. They show that these animals belong to a separate group.

Both rabbits and hares have long ears and long hind legs. But wild hares generally are larger than rabbits, and their ears and

106

Angora rabbit (left) and Belgian Hare (right).

legs are even longer. Baby hares also are covered with fur when they are born, and their eyes are open. Newborn rabbits have no fur, and their eyes are closed. The mother hare makes no nest for her young ones, but Mother Rabbit digs a shallow nest and lines it with fur from her own body. Her little ones do not leave the nest until they are 10 or 12 days old.

Wild hares and rabbits live in almost all parts of the world. They are easily tamed, and no one knows who first domesticated them. But ancient Romans ate rabbit meat and raised the animals on farms. Today many meat markets sell "dressed" rabbits, and people often raise the animals in backyards. Rabbit meat is light-colored and tastes just a bit like chicken.

Rabbits are the most important fur-bearing animals. Every year, more than 100 million rabbit skins are made into fur coats, fur trimmings for cloth coats and dresses, glove linings, and felt hats. The fur is dyed various colors and is sold under made-up names such as Baltic Fox, Belgian Beaver, Hudson Seal, though in the United States the fur must be labeled rabbit.

Although there are several kinds of wild rabbits and hares

in North America, our domestic rabbits originally came from Europe. They belong to six principal breeds, only one of which was developed in the United States.

The Belgian Hare looks like a hare, but it really is a rabbit. It is a reddish-tan animal with ears about five inches long and a rather long, straight tail. It weighs about eight pounds. Some people say this breed began when wild hares that lived in Belgium were crossed with domestic rabbits. Others say the animals are a special type of rabbit that was bred to look like a wild English hare.

The New Zealand breed does not come from New Zealand. It was developed in various parts of the United States, and its ancestors were Belgian Hares. New Zealand rabbits are small animals that have white or brownish-red coats and weigh 9 to 13 pounds when they are fully grown. Some rabbit fanciers would like to change the name from New Zealand to American Red, although many of these animals are white.

The Flemish Giant is our largest rabbit, for it sometimes

White New Zealand rabbit (left) and a Flemish Giant (right)

weighs 20 pounds. Flemish Giants were developed in the part of Belgium called Flanders. The first animals were gray, but colors now range from white to fawn, blue-gray, and black. The animals take a year or even 14 months to become full grown.

The Chinchilla breed was developed in France and was brought to America in about 1918. Three slightly different varieties range in weight from 6 to 12 or 13 pounds. Chinchilla rabbits were bred for their thick pearl-gray fur. It resembles that of the real chinchilla, a long-tailed rodent from South America whose fur is much more expensive than mink.

The Champagne (sham pane´) breed also comes from France. The babies are born black, but their outer fur turns silvery white over a dark gray undercoat.

The Angora breed probably came from Turkey, but it was raised in France for many years. From France it was taken to England, and then to the United States. Angora rabbits weigh 6 to 8 pounds and their colors range from white to blue-gray, fawn, and black. The animals are covered with fluffy wool about three inches long, and they are sheared every two or three months. Each rabbit produces 12 to 16 ounces of wool in one year. The wool is used to make cloth for very fine dresses and coats. Since Angora wool is very expensive, it is generally mixed with less costly wool from sheep.

In the Arctic—Reindeer and Musk Oxen

A HERD of reindeer walked across a rolling plain in Lapland. In a few places the ground was bare, but most of it was covered with snow. The deer's hoofs left broad, curved tracks as the animals walked across the snow.

Most deer are wild animals, but these reindeer were domesticated. They belonged to two families of people called Lapps. The Lapps had spent the winter in wooden houses near the edge of a forest, where the deer were sheltered from storms. But when spring came the people left their houses and began to travel northward. They were taking the deer to their summer pasture near the shore of the Arctic Ocean.

Many deer had nothing to do but walk. Others carried packs that were tied to their backs. Still other deer pulled boat-shaped sleds, which the Lapps call "pulkas." Some pulkas were piled high with tents, bedding, pots for cooking and for coffee, and other household goods. Other pulkas carried women, several babies, and some grandfathers and grandmothers who could not walk very far. Children with red coats and woolen caps ran beside the sleds. Men and big boys with dogs followed the herd to keep the deer from lagging or wandering away on the plain.

In the Far North, when summer draws near, the sun rises

above the horizon and does not set for weeks. At first the sunshine is dull and cool, but it soon becomes brighter and warmer. At last it begins to melt the snow. This uncovers bushes and other small plants that grow close to the ground.

The man who was leader of the Lapps kept watch for a broad southern slope on which most of the snow had melted. When he saw one, he pointed to it and shouted some words that meant, "This is the place to stop!" The other men answered, "All right," and began to turn the reindeer. When the animals came to the plant-covered slope, they began to feed.

Many deer feed on grass and the tender tips of bushes. Rein-

This domestic reindeer has antlers with many branches.

deer like these things, too, but their favorite food is a bluish-gray plant known as "reindeer moss." It really is a lichen (ly' ken), related to the thin, dry lichens that grow on rocks and trees.

While the deer munched their "moss," the Lapp women put up tents, made beds on the ground, and began to cook. The men selected milking deer from the herd, so the children could have milk with their meal. After supper the grandparents told stories, and then almost everyone went to bed. Only a few men and older boys stayed awake to watch over the reindeer and keep them from wandering away.

.　.　.

Reindeer now live in cold regions on the tundra from Norway to Siberia and from islands in the Arctic Ocean to Eastern Russia. Many also live in woods among high mountains. They thrive in the forests of the Ural Mountains and in the region around Lake Baykal in southern Siberia. Long ago during the Ice Age, the deer ranged across Germany and into southern France. There they were killed and eaten by Stone-Age hunters who lived in shallow caves. Some of these hunters also painted pictures of the deer, just as they painted pictures of horses, bison, cattle, and other wild animals.

Although ancient hunters of France killed reindeer, they did not domesticate the animals. This was probably done first by the Samoyeds, a Siberian-Mongolian people in the Baykal area. These people trained the deer as they did horses and cattle and used them for riding, pack, and draft animals. They probably took the domesticated forest deer to Europe, where they developed into the tundra deer of the modern Lapps.

112

By the end of the fifth century in China, domesticated reindeer were being driven and milked. The Norsmen of the ninth century left records of tame deer. And before the tenth century domestic reindeer were drawing sleds carrying three or four persons in the area southeast of Lake Baykal, and people there made clothes of the animal skins.

Today the Lapps depend on their reindeer for meat, milk, cheese, and skins. Wealth of these people is reckoned by the number of deer owned. In Finland, reindeer meat is considered a great delicacy and brings a high price.

Wild reindeer grow four to five feet high at the shoulder and weigh as much as 300 pounds. They have heavy bodies and rather short legs, with broad hoofs and hairy feet that do not sink into the snow. The nose is covered with soft furry hair, and coarse hair on neck and body covers a woolly undercoat. The head and neck are almost white, but the rest of the coat is brownish gray and brown.

Both male and female reindeer have antlers. Those of the female are small, but the male's antlers grow large and branch several times. The strongest, healthiest deer have the largest antlers.

Most domestic reindeer are smaller than wild ones, though they are strong enough to pull loads of 300 pounds at 8 to 10 miles an hour. One special breed raised in Siberia is larger than domestic reindeer of Europe. This big deer is more often ridden than hitched to a sled.

Wild reindeer of North America are known as caribou (kar' i boo). Caribou of several kinds once ranged from Alaska to Newfoundland, and from Greenland to Idaho and Wiscon-

113

sin. In many places they have been killed by hunters. But there still are large herds in Alaska and northern Canada.

Besides caribou, a few herds of domestic reindeer now live in Alaska. They are descendants of animals brought from Siberia by the United States Government, which hired Lapp herders to teach Eskimos to care for the animals. For a time the herds were handled with some success, but by 1969 only 30,000 domestic reindeer were left in western Alaska.

In 1929 the Canadian Government bought 3,000 Alaskan reindeer to provide food and clothing for Eskimos in the Northwest Territories. These people also were trained to take care of the deer by herders who came from Lapland.

The only other country in which reindeer are kept is Iceland. The animals were taken there in 1870. They have done very well, although the climate is much warmer than the climate of Lapland, northern Alaska, or northwestern Canada.

A Stone-age picture of two fighting reindeer. From a cave in France.

Although reindeer have been domesticated for nearly 1,500 years the musk ox, another Arctic animal, was first tamed less than 20 years ago. The musk ox was once believed to be half sheep and half cattle, but it is truly related to neither. Its closest living relatives are goats and perhaps antelopes or even bison. Eskimos call it *Oomigmak*, "the bearded one." It is a powerful, shaggy animal with long curved horns. The bulls measure about five feet at the shoulder and weigh 700 to 800 pounds. Great coats of hair with thick blankets of underwool make the creatures look even bigger. This wool is the chief economic value of the animal.

The wool, known as *Qiviut*, a registered trademark, is very light and will not shrink when scrubbed or boiled. It takes natural dyes and can be knitted into soft, warm garments.

Each spring the underwool loosens naturally and begins to work its way through the long outer guardhairs until it hangs off the animal in large sheets, which are easily plucked. The shedding takes three to four weeks. It is hoped by selective breeding to increase the Qiviut yield. Already the best mature bulls shed 6½ pounds a year and should continue to produce wool for 20 years. After being cleaned, a pound can be spun into a strand of yarn 10 miles long.

Once widely distributed in the Far North, the "bearded ones" were pushed southward during the Ice Age, and in central Europe, like reindeer, were hunted by early man. They became extinct in the Old World in prehistoric times and today only about 10,000 are left in herds in northern Canada and 6,000 in Greenland. The Canadian Government has protected its remaining herds since 1926 and requires permits even to capture wild animals alive.

Domestication of the animals began in 1954 in Vermont. Here captured wild calves were tamed and produced young. The animals are intelligent and adapt readily to farm life. They need no barns and eat much less than cattle do. They can forage for themselves for their favorite food of leaves and tender willow shoots. In winter they reach grasses by breaking through deep snow with their broad front hoofs. They "drink" snow when thirsty.

After 10 years of study in Vermont, the Institute of Northern Agricultural Research started the first breeding station for domestic oxen at a farm close to the University of Alaska campus. From 33 wild animals captured in 1964 and 1965, a herd of 94 has been built up. On the basis of this domestic herd, the Institute established the Musk Ox Project in collaboration with the University and the W. K. Kellogg Foundation. The purpose is to develop an industry from which Arctic people can derive income by working with the musk oxen or with the wool. Plans are to locate a substation near an Eskimo village where native herdsmen will be trained to run the station as members of a cooperative. The women members are all Eskimos trained by the project staff to hand-knit the Qiviut.

In addition to the Alaskan establishment and one at Fort Chimo in northern Quebec, the Institute has a new station in northern Norway and plans to operate also in southwest Greenland, Iceland, and Canada's Northwest Territories.

Elephants

AKBAR, a tame elephant, walked toward a range of forested hills in northern India. A white official who had charge of wild animals sat on a thick pad of burlap fastened to Akbar's back. An Indian driver, or mahout, rode on the elephant's neck. The mahout had a stick with a steel point and hook. He used the stick and his bare feet to guide Akbar.

The white man, Akbar, and his mahout were going to an elephant drive. This drive would take place in a forest, and there was still a long way to go. The mahout prodded Akbar's shoulder lightly with the point of his stick. This told the elephant to take longer, swifter steps. By doing this, the big animal traveled as fast as a horse could trot.

After hurrying for several miles, Akbar came to a lowland covered with coarse elephant grass that grew higher than his head. There, the elephant could not go so fast. With his trunk, he pushed the tall stalks aside so that they did not touch the two men. He went still more slowly in a swamp, testing the ground before each step. Elephants do not mind mud, but they make sure that the ground under it is firm.

Beyond the swamp was a stream with steep, slippery banks. Akbar braced his forelegs, sat on his haunches, and slid into the water. There he stood up and began to wade. Elephants are good swimmers, but this stream was so shallow that Akbar could wade it easily.

Men who were preparing for the elephant drive had camped on the farther bank of the stream. Some had built simple shelters on the ground. Others lived in bamboo huts built on posts five or six feet high. The floors of these huts stayed dry, even after long, hard rains.

When Akbar came to the camp, he knelt to let the official get down from his back. Other men loosened the pad of burlap and let it roll to the ground. Then the mahout tapped Akbar's cheek. "Get up, great one," said the man. "It is time to drink and take your bath."

Akbar slid down the bank, dipped his trunk into the stream, and sucked until his trunk was full. Then he put its tip between his lips and squirted the water into his mouth. He did this again and again, until his stomach was so full of water that his sides began to bulge.

Elephants can bathe by filling their trunks with water, which they squirt over their backs. Akbar did this several times, and then he lay down in the stream. His mahout waded out to him and scrubbed the beast's sides with a stone. This stone was rough, and it took off the dead outer layers of skin which make many elephants look brown instead of blackish gray. Akbar looked and felt very clean when he left the stream to wait for elephants and workmen to come back to the camp. Next day, Akbar and his mahout would help them get ready for the drive.

Elephant drives are held because these big animals are not raised on farms, like cattle and horses. When people want ele-

Asiatic elephants have bulging "foreheads" and rather small ears.

phants for work or to show in circuses or zoos, wild ones must be captured and trained to do what people tell them.

A successful elephant drive takes a great deal of work and planning. First, men and trained elephants build a corral, or keddah. The men cut down trees and saw them into logs. Elephants haul the logs to the place where the keddah is being built. There, other men tie the logs and brace them firmly. A keddah requires hundreds or even thousands of logs, which are tied together with tons and tons of rope.

When the keddah is built, hundreds of men are hired to work as "beaters." Trackers meanwhile search through the forest until they find a wild elephant herd. Then the beaters spread out in a C-shaped or U-shaped line six to eight miles long. The men shout, beat drums, or pound on dry lengths of bamboo. At night they build small fires, which make little spots of light all along the line.

Noise and fires disturb the wild elephants, which try to slip away. But as the animals move, the men follow, building new fires and making more noise. They do this day after day and night after night, guiding the herd into the keddah. Then a log gate is closed to keep the elephants from getting out.

Twenty elephants went into the keddah which Akbar and his mahout helped to build. At first the animals trumpeted loudly and pushed against the sides of the keddah. Later, when the animals became quiet, the man who was in charge of the drive chose the ones that were to be kept and trained.

Since young elephants can be tamed more easily than old ones, only young ones were chosen. Two mahouts rode their tame elephants into the keddah. They went close to each side of a young, wild animal and tied him to a tree with ropes. When all the young animals were tied, other men opened the gate and let the older elephants go back into the forest.

As soon as the old elephants had gone, the mahouts began to train the young ones. They were taught to stand beside tame animals, such as Akbar, and then to walk behind them. The young animals also became friends with their mahouts, who fed them, scrubbed their backs, and picked splinters and sharp stones out of their feet. Soon the elephants became so fond of their mahouts that they wanted to stay with them instead of going back to the herd.

. . .

Wild elephant herds contain 15 to 30 animals, all of which belong to one family. They feed, sleep, and bathe in the day-time, and feed or travel at night. Elephants can sleep standing up, as horses do, but they sometimes lie on their sides. When an elephant lies down, it curls its trunk close to its mouth, out of harm's way.

Mother elephants generally have one baby at a time — twins are very rare. The little one is about three feet tall and weighs 180 to 200 pounds. It has a thin coat of coarse black hair, and its trunk is short and stiff. It drinks milk with its mouth and grows rapidly. In a year it becomes more than four feet high and weighs about 450 pounds.

People used to think that elephants lived to be very old — as old as 200 years. We now know that these big animals have shorter lives than human beings. An elephant matures when it is 15 to 18 years old, though it keeps on growing for many years more. At 40 it is middle-aged, and the upper edges of its ears start to fold downward. The animal becomes old before it is 60, though healthy animals live several years longer. Very few elephants become more than 80 years old.

These facts describe Asiatic elephants. This is the species to which Akbar belonged, and the one we see most often in zoos and circuses. Asiatic elephants range from India to the Malay Peninsula and live on islands such as Ceylon, Sumatra, and Borneo. The animals become 7 to 10 feet high at the shoulder

An old Asiatic elephant has hollows above the eyes and downturned edges on the ears. This one is almost 60 years old. An African elephant can be recognized by its big ears and rounded "forehead."

African Elephant

Asiatic Elephant

and weigh 4,500 to 10,000 pounds. There is a hollow above the eyes, but the "forehead" bulges. The ears are not very large, nor are the tusks. Many of the females have no tusks.

One kind of African elephant is so small that we call it a pigmy, but another species sometimes becomes 11 feet in height. The front of its head is smoothly curved, and the ears are very large. The tusks grow much larger than those of the Asian species. Some tusks of African elephants are 10 feet long and weigh 225 pounds.

Elephants often seem to be very intelligent, and in some ways they are. They learn tricks and understand commands, they remember for months or years, and they often do difficult things which no one has taught them. They will work hard to get what they want, and they find clever ways to keep from doing things they do not like to do.

Elephants also have good-sized brains. The brain of a 4-ton elephant weighs almost 10 pounds, which is more than three times as much as the brain of a human being. But the elephant's brain is not as good as ours, and it cannot think nearly so well. Perhaps the animals seem more intelligent than they are because they are big and strong and have trunks.

We often think of the elephant's trunk as its nose, for the animal breathes and smells with it. Actually, the trunk contains the nose, upper lip, and part of both cheeks. All these form a very special organ that becomes six to seven feet long and contains about 30,000 muscles. These muscles stretch the trunk out, roll it up, and move it in almost any direction. They work swiftly or very slowly, producing violent movements and others that are delicate and precise.

Elephants use their trunks as weapons against human beings or other animals. As we have seen, they also drink with their trunks and use them as shower baths or sprays. Any elephant older than a baby also uses its trunk for feeding. The animal breaks branches from trees, pulls grass, picks up hay, and holds things as small as peanuts. A full-grown elephant puts about 200 pounds of food into its mouth every day by means of its trunk.

·   ·   ·

Most elephants work willingly after they have been trained. A work elephant can carry 1,000 pounds in a boxlike or basketlike saddle fastened to its back. In harness the animal pulls logs weighing as much as four tons. If the logs sink into mud or sand, the elephant pries them out with his tusks or the base of his trunk. Before tractors and trucks became common, circus elephants often pushed or pulled heavy wagons. Even now you may see elephants pushing trucks and heavy wagons that get stuck in muddy ground.

In ancient times, elephants were used for warfare as well as for work. No one knows just when this custom began, but Asiatic elephants were trained to fight before Alexander the Great went to India. That was about 400 years before Jesus was born. The animals carried supplies or soldiers armed with spears, and they often battered down defenses. Archers advanced behind armored elephants, just as modern infantrymen advance behind big armored tanks.

Roman soldiers first met war elephants more than 2,200 years ago, in a battle with a Macedonian army. The Romans ran when they saw the big gray beasts, but in time the Roman army got an elephant squadron of its own. The animals were not afraid to fight, but they sometimes became so excited that they trampled on soldiers of their own army, not on the enemy.

About 2,200 years ago, the Romans learned about wild animal circuses from soldiers who had been in Asia. But the Roman circus was not a place where animals were shown in cages or performed in rings. In the Roman circus the animals fought with each other or with men called gladiators. Elephants fought other elephants or rhinoceros, lions, and even big dogs. One Roman emperor also had elephants hitched to chariots, so they could race like horses.

It is said that Julius Caesar took an elephant to England more than 2,000 years ago. An English circus had one performing elephant early in the 1700's. The first elephant in the United States was brought to Salem, Massachusetts, in 1796. The animal was sold for $10,000, and was bought by a man who exhibited it in New York, Philadelphia, and many other cities. Grown-ups paid 50 cents to see this "monster," but children looked at it for a quarter. In time, every circus had at least one elephant, and some had more than 20. Sixty was the largest number of elephants ever shown in one performance.

Although elephants have been tamed since ancient times, they have not been domesticated. This is because baby elephants are hard to raise and take a long time to grow up. It is easier to capture young wild elephants and tame them than it is to breed grown animals and then raise their young ones. But the tamed animals remain wild, even though they live with human beings during most of their lives.

Index

This index lists all illustrations, as well as the pages on which descriptions of the animals begin.